Andrew Johnson
and the
Uses of
Constitutional Power

James E. Sefton

Andrew Johnson
and the
Uses of
Constitutional Power

Edited by Oscar Handlin

Little, Brown and Company · *Boston* · *Toronto*

PRINTED IN THE UNITED STATES OF AMERICA

for
Brainerd Dyer
and
Eugene N. Anderson

retired as professors
but still on active duty as friends

Editor's Preface

A CRUEL turn of fate brought Andrew Johnson into the White House. No doubt any successor to Abraham Lincoln would have found the presidency demanding, but the shock of the assassination and the unexpectedness of the succession compounded Johnson's difficulties.

The United States in 1865 had just emerged from four years of destructive war. A good part of the country lay devastated, and sectional and racial hatreds blocked the way to reconciliation. Yet the nation could not focus on the problems inherited from the past, for it had already entered a new era. Since the middle of the nineteenth century, transcontinental expansion, the development of national markets, and industrialization had transformed the society in which Americans lived, so that there could be no expectation of a return to the past after the peace.

Above all, the President in 1865 confronted the perplexing problems of the freedmen. Questions not resolved by the war, by the Emancipation Proclamation, or even by the Thirteenth Amendment called for answers. Was it enough to declare these people legally free without supplying them with the means by which to sustain themselves? Were they to sink into a peonage hardly different from slavery? Did legal freedom also imply political and social equality? Even the administration of the martyred President had no easy solution to these problems. Johnson was sadly unprepared by temperament or experience for leadership in the crisis.

Neither the courts nor Congress could settle these matters, which were not constitutional, not even purely political, but, in the broadest sense of the term, philosophical. They involved the definition of equality and of citizenship. Since the Dred Scott decision the public's esteem of the courts was not high; and Congress was an incomplete body, as yet representing only part of the country. The inability of the judiciary and the legislature to secure the consent of the governed left the task to the President. Lincoln had managed — partly by willingness to use emergency wartime power, partly by enlistment of patriotic sentiment for union, and partly by the understanding of humanity that made him a superb politician.

There were parallels between Andrew Johnson's background and that of Abraham Lincoln. Johnson had been a small-scale businessman, close to the yeomen of Tennessee, self-educated and self-made. His ideals were those of an earlier America about to be displaced by new social and political forces. The absorbing story of his efforts to apply those ideals to new conditions reveals the forces at work in the nation at large.

OSCAR HANDLIN

Author's Preface

To KNOW the essential outlines of Andrew Johnson's life is to appreciate that he caused trouble for many of his contemporaries, who found him rigid, intractable, sometimes crude, often wrongheaded, and often courageous. He also causes trouble for historians, who recognize the same qualities as his contemporaries. The biographer of Johnson might adopt a number of themes to explain his life, such as Johnson the anomalous southerner, Johnson the Unionist, or Johnson the antielitist. Of the themes that bear particularly on his presidency, the uses of constitutional power seems especially appropriate. It relates his presidency to his prior experiences and preserves the unity of a whole life in which the early years, less well known than they should be, strongly shaped his later views. The theme of constitutional power also offers the reader the challenge of coping with Johnson on his own ground and understanding (though not necessarily liking or approving) him on his own terms. Finally, this theme uses Johnson's career to illustrate one of the central tensions in American political and institutional history of the middle period. The theme is by its nature very broad and hardly limited to, or even necessarily characterized by, the narrow question of how a lawyer might interpret a particular word or phrase of law. Many political events have a constitutional dimension. This volume therefore retains a strong narrative core to emphasize that a public figure's constitutional views take shape and receive expression in the course of his government service.

This volume has been a long time in the making. Besides the

many people at Little, Brown and Company, especially Marian Ferguson, who have contributed to its completion, certain others deserve mention. As series editor, Professor Oscar Handlin offered constructive suggestions for improving the manuscript. Professor James C. Curtis brought the experience of his own effort for this series to bear on the early chapters, and Professor Ralph Haskins read the entire manuscript with great care. My colleague Professor Michael Patterson also read the entire manuscript, and others allowed their path past my door to be waylaid by questions and chats. At a very early stage the Penrose Fund of the American Philosophical Society provided a small research grant, and two former students, Stephen C. Bedau and Stephen D. Hartman, transcribed some drafts of proclamations and messages. Charlotte Oyer and Donald Read of the California State University, Northridge, library tracked down elusive things on interlibrary loan. Maxine Chadwick and Nancy Meadows of our department staff helped with typing and Xeroxing. My students have contributed in their own special way with their hallway greetings and the inquiry of how was "Andy" coming along; those who, for their senior research projects, wrote biographies of hitherto unbiographed Civil War generals while I was writing this work shared some of the pleasures and frustrations — and when they realized I was writing for an unfootnoted series, they mirthfully accused me of "doing things the easy way." Professor Brainerd Dyer listened to parts of the story and made his usual helpful suggestions, and Professor Eugene Anderson always wanted to know the latest during my visits. My dedication of this volume to them expresses my appreciation and respect over the years. Finally, some of the better parts of this volume were written on my mother's dining-room table during periodic pleasant visits to her little home.

JAMES E. SEFTON

San Fernando Valley, California
Spring 1979

Contents

Contents

I

In Search of
a Greeneville
1808–1835

IF ANYONE, during that Christmas season of 1808, had told a gathering of national political figures that in 1865 the President of the United States would be the young lad just born in poverty in North Carolina, they would have snorted with amusement. Greater still would have been their astonishment to hear that he would assume office upon the assassination of his predecessor, also to be born in poverty two months later that winter and a little more than 500 miles distant. Assassination was the way of things in decadent European states, not in the vigorous young republic that had crested the Appalachians, strode to the Mississippi, and, with the assistance of a recent fortuitous purchase in Paris, placed itself on the slopes of the Rockies. Indeed, there were to be no actual presidential assassinations in American history until that of Lincoln and only one unsuccessful attempt.

As for poor boys becoming president, that too in 1808 was an improbable turn of events. The Constitution, as yet only twenty years old, did not prohibit such a thing, yet seemed to militate against it, with an electoral college rather than direct election, and voting qualifications left to the states. A small percentage of the adult population took part in politics, and even when people of modest means did participate, they accepted the popular hallmarks of fitness for office and voted for men of substance and repute.

Certainly the experience of the country thus far raised few concerns about the future of the presidency. The current occupant of the Executive Mansion, Thomas Jefferson, would shortly retire to the comparative comforts of Monticello to contemplate and philosophize. His already elected successor, the highly experienced James Madison, owed his nomination to the congressonal caucus, the safe and standard method. Before them had come George Washington and John Adams, cut from similar molds. Surely a poor lad, without formal schooling and with only a tailor's trade, could not hope to follow in such exalted footsteps.

Yet the first half of the nineteenth century recast roles so that a new breed of player shouldered into the spotlight. Jacksonian democracy represented a surge of popular influence and participation by the common man in the affairs of government. New western states came into the Union, and older ones revised their constitutions. Restrictions on voting and office holding loosened. The clubbish party caucus gave way to the raucous national party nominating convention. With the party platform, perhaps an invention of the political faction supporting Clinton for president in 1812 but certainly not standard until the 1840s, came the opportunity to measure candidates against professed principles.

In such an environment, presidential elections took on more vivid colors. So great was the Jacksonian democratic emphasis on the "common" voter that the canvass of 1840 saw the Whig opposition convert the well-born, aristocratic, and proper William Henry Harrison into a rough-and-tumble, cider-guzzling, dawn-to-dusk plowman as a means of attracting votes. At the same time, the Whigs painted Democratic Martin Van Buren, who actually had sprung from humble origins, as a foppish aristocrat who fiddled while the country burned during the panic of 1837. Principles gave place to slogans, and the level of nonsense reached in that campaign would have horrified the proper gentlemen of 1808.

Other strange things were to come. In 1844 "Little Jimmy Polk from Duck River," as some contemporaries derisively called him, could run as the "dark horse," and defeat Henry Clay, one of the nation's foremost statesmen, although winning less than half of all popular votes cast. In 1852 the bland, monochromatic Franklin Pierce would defeat the nation's number-one war hero, "Fuss and Feathers" Winfield Scott. But perhaps the least probable affair of all would develop in the midst of a great civil war, when the two lads born in poverty in that winter of 1808–09 found themselves sharing a successful presidential ticket, pledged to save the Union and elected by all who rallied round the standard, be they northern patriot or southern loyalist, ex-Whig or War Democrat, abolitionist or racial skeptic.

The Civil War and Reconstruction represented the ultimate clash over constitutional power in America, the combustion of a pile of philosophical kindling that grew ever larger as the political life of Andrew Johnson progressed. The principal issues that engaged the national attention from the 1820s until 1860—the tariff, expansion and western land policy, federal aid to transportation and other internal improvements, a national bank, expansion or limitation of slavery—all evoked bitter debate over one central question: the desirable functions of government. Considered in the context of a federal system, under a Constitution that, with varying degrees of clarity, assigned powers to national and state levels, the issues fueled growing controversies about the nature of the Constitution and the Union. In the America of Andrew Johnson's youth and political novitiate the federal government kept within a narrow and traditional compass; in the America of his maturity and political seniority the needs and results of Civil War propelled the federal government into unfamiliar functions and renewed constitutional controversy. Moreover, between Jackson and Lincoln, the presidency took a generally subordinate role to Congress in the national government, a status the restless, ambitious Johnson never particularly liked. At first only an observer of events, and one not likely to travel beyond the confines of local politics, Johnson carved out a career that brought him to the very center of conflict over the uses of constitutional power. Moreover, during his own presidency, his views on questions of constitutional power came to be so out of harmony with those prevailing in Congress that Johnson, who until that time had lost only one popular election in his life, came within one vote of removal from office.

In 1808, however, all of these things were but shadows on the shore dimly seen. For the moment, Mary McDonough Johnson was giving birth to her second son, and the circumstances did not augur particularly well. Mary and her immigrant husband of seven years, Jacob, both illiterate, were the hired hands at a tavern in Raleigh. The place was a prominent and well-reputed hostelry, located on a main road hard by the state capitol, and it catered especially to traveling lawyers, merchants, and others of similar station. Although Raleigh itself was hardly an elegant southern city, class distinctions prevailed, and these wayfarers clearly looked down on the Johnsons as poor whites.

Andrew was the third child, born when his father was thirty and his mother twenty-five. The first son, William, came in 1804, and a daughter, Elizabeth, born in 1806, died in infancy. Andrew was the last of the Johnson children, for in the winter of 1811 Jacob contracted a fatal case of pneumonia from plunging into a frigid creek to rescue several friends whose drunken carelessness caused their boat to overturn. Mary, left to support an eight-year-old and a toddler not yet four, was in desperate straits. Reluctant to throw herself on the charity of the neighborhood, she obtained a loom to support her family by weaving. She might have succeeded, too, but for the unlucky selection of a second husband. About two years after

Jacob's death, she married Turner Doughtry, also a poor white but no match for the children's father as a provider or head of household. His shiftlessness and irresponsibility left the family in worse straits than before.

For the next few years, when the children of better-situated families dutifully attended to the assignments of private tutors —for Raleigh had no public schools—Andy was out vagabonding and acquiring a more worldly education. He did odd jobs around the tavern, accepting whatever tips were to be had, but much of the time he roamed on his own, impressing the other boys with his dauntless spirit and his thirst for adventure. Mary's concern that her boys were growing up with neither education nor trade, and the continued worthlessness of Turner Doughtry, brought her to the decision, in 1822, to apprentice both Andy and Bill to a Raleigh tailor, James J. Selby.

It is curiously appropriate that the two oldest extant documents bearing directly on the youth of Andrew Johnson, well known in manhood for an indomitable, even intractable character, should be the instrument of his apprenticeship and a newspaper notice by his new master identifying him as a runaway. At first Andy was not at all averse to the idea of being apprenticed so that he could help support the family, learn a trade, and get the rudiments of an education. Selby appears to have kept his part of the bargain. He taught Andy the tailor's craft and paid his support, though the boy continued to live at home. Andy learned quickly and gave satisfacton with his work. Selby's tailor shop was not merely Andy's trade school but his makeshift grammar school besides. Handicraft shops of the day kept long and tiresome hours, and to relieve the tedium, literate visitors often spent a while reading to the workmen from newspapers or collections of essays. At Selby's this was the function sometimes of the foreman, James Litchford, and sometimes of Dr. William G. Hill, an educated townsman. Such an arrangement suited Andy just fine, and one may well imagine a few inadvertent needle pricks or burns with a hot goose as the boy listened attentively to the words of famous statesmen, British and American, historic and modern.

How was it that a teenage country boy, the captain—after hours, at least—of his daredevil friends, did not rebel at such heavy stuff? The answer is probably subjective: a natural inquisitiveness, the challenge of learning, and the dramatic oral presentation to which the material lent itself. Or so, at least, Johnson's friends testified years afterward when memories, embellished by his later career, provided the stories that take the place of hard evidence concerning an obscure childhood.

Not content to be a passive listener, Andy had to read for himself. Doubtless with the help of Litchford and Hill he learned to decipher words; the rules of spelling and the function of grammar remained mysteries until several years later when he finally learned to write. For his remarkable perseverance and accomplishments, Hill rewarded the lad with a copy of the *Speaker*, from which he had often read, and for forty years Andrew treasured the little book, it being finally lost when the Confederate government confiscated his Tennessee home.

The apprenticeship to Selby was a milestone in young Andrew's life. Without the practical training and rudimentary education he would have had no prospects. Yet he did have some misgivings. Corporal punishment for infractions was well within the law, and although there is no direct evidence of brutality, Andrew later recalled Selby as a harsh and overbearing man. Such a disposition was bound to grate on the proud and independent youth, especially if he had to endure it until age twenty-one. In addition, Andrew was ever the rascally teenager, and now that he was an apprentice, his ideas of fun had serious consequences when they brought him afoul of the law. In June 1824, a little over two years after the indenture began, matters came to a head, and Andrew ran away.

Popular accounts claimed that he and another apprentice were caught throwing rocks at the house of a woman in town either for the purpose of vexing her or teasing her daughters. The irate woman threatened to report them, and so four youths (Andrew and his friend having secured the pledge of Andrew's brother William and another apprentice) set off on the night of June 15, now quite outside the law regardless of how the "chunkin'" incident might have turned out.

Selby quickly announced the caper in the Raleigh *Star* and offered a reward for the two fugitives who were his own apprentices. The Johnson brothers commanded $10 as a pair, but Selby was willing to give the same reward for "Andrew Johnson alone." Had the boys actually read the notice, they would have howled with delight, for somehow their physical descriptions had got reversed, and Andrew, of "dark complexion, black hair, eyes, and habits," had been given William's "very fleshy, freckled face, light hair, and fair complexion."

The runaways took the south road out of Raleigh, and the first long stopover of their Huckleberry Finn escapade found them in the little hamlet of Carthage, about 50 miles below the capital. There they employed needle and thread as a means of support. Work aplenty found its way to their claptrap lodging, but security still raised nagging doubts. Again the south road beckoned, and this time their trek ended across the line in Laurens, South Carolina, where Selby's legal threats had no force. Winter had now set in, and the weather discouraged further travel. Female companionship had the same effect, and during his sojourn in Laurens the sixteen-year-old Andrew fell in love with a beautiful girl named Sara Word. If her affection matched Andrew's, her mettle did not, and she acquiesced in her parents' peremptory ruling that a union between belle and mudsill was not to be.

Frustrated, concerned about his mother, and anxious to settle his legal relations with Selby, Andrew decided to return to Raleigh in the autumn of 1825. But Selby, perverse, would not release him from his agreement, nor would he take him back, which meant that for another four years no craftsman in the state would be willing to hire the youth, and even if he set himself up in business, Selby might fetch the law upon him at any moment.

The closure of all avenues of improvement, the ease with

which self-selected betters oppressed those striving to improve themselves, and Raleigh's pretensions to southern elegance all brought to the fore a fierce, lifelong pride and self-respect. A permanent relocation seemed in order. William had already moved west across the mountains to the Sequatchie Valley of southeastern Tennessee; perhaps in that new state, where many Carolinians had found success, Andrew might find the freedom and opportunity he sought.

At seventeen, Andrew Johnson trod the path of thousands, more, of millions, along one of the great mainstreams of American national development. The West was the land of opportunity, where a man poor in worldly goods but rich in skills and strength of character could overcome adversity and prosper. Andrew dreamed the nineteenth-century dream, and he possessed the qualities to make it come true. Moving in the first half of the nineteenth century was more a declaration of faith in self than a process of successful extrication from previous identification. For life, although hard, was hedged about with few administrative classifications, and one could wend his way across the Appalachians — or the Mississippi or the Great Plains — without leaving behind a trail of telltale paper. Thus began a westward odyssey that lasted a year and covered 500 miles through eastern and middle Tennessee and northern Alabama.

In the summer of 1826 reports reached Andrew that his mother, still burdened with the ne'er-do-well Turner Doughtry, could hardly make ends meet. He went back to Raleigh and concluded that his mother and Doughtry should return with him to Tennessee. Moving the household was not a large task. Some oddments of ratty furniture, fit more for kindling wood, and some other domestic items were all the belongings the Johnsons possessed. These they placed in a rude two-wheeled cart in the charge of a blind, undernourished little pony. Thus inauspiciously, in August 1826, began the second Johnson trek across the mountains. Not yet eighteen, Andrew shouldered the responsibility of head of the family.

Whatever the intended destination, events dictated otherwise. At the end of a particularly wearying day in September, the travelers came to the village of Greeneville, which, with its mill, spring, cool greenery, and pleasant if dusty streets, offered a welcome place for a short rest. On their entrance into the town Johnson noticed a girl approximately his own age and asked if she knew of any lodgings. Eliza McArdle, whose neat and pretty appearance contrasted sharply with the youth's grubby disarray, took the party to a storekeeper who had a spare cottage. Both of them, or so it was told in the traditional and well-colored stories of East Tennessee, had an early inkling that they would one day be married. Six weeks later the Johnsons moved on 40 miles to Rutledge. In the spring of 1827 Greeneville's only tailor left town, and when Johnson heard the news, he decided to return to Greene County. Greeneville had more population than Rutledge, and from March 1827 onward there would be no place called home but Greeneville.

Andrew Johnson established himself as a citizen of Tennessee at a time of steady growth in that state. The first permanent settlers had put down roots just before the Revolution, and in 1796 the area severed itself from North Carolina to become the Union's sixteenth state. Tennessee was at once a southern and a western state; at once raw frontier and refined plantation; at once the home of subsistence farmers and great cotton magnates. The jostling of competing social and economic values gave state politics contours that were at least exciting, though at times difficult to follow. East Tennessee, an area of mountain ridges and river valleys, was fertile but not suitable for the large-scale agriculture typical of middle and west Tennessee. Thus it was the domain of independent, subsistence farmers. Tobacco grew well enough in some areas to be marketable, while other residents grew garden truck, raised livestock, or made cloth on their own looms. Slaves were few, forming less than 10 percent of the population, and that small number represented household servants or single farmhands. In earlier years east Tennessee had been the dominant section of the state, but by the time Johnson arrived, Knoxville was no longer the capital and much of the power and influence had shifted westward. The economy, however, never dependent on cotton, remained stable even in the uncertain period of the panic of 1819.

Greeneville had shared in the general stability of cast Tennessee, and it was a good town in which to set up shop and establish a family. In May 1827 Johnson married Eliza McArdle. Their youth—he was eighteen and she seventeen—and their mutual affection gave the marriage a solid foundation on which difficulties as well as joys would be shared together. Eliza's background, in contrast to Johnson's first amorous venture in Laurens, ensured a marriage free of carping in-laws. Her father had been a shoemaker, and since his death Eliza had lived with her mother, helping to maintain the household by making sandals and quilts. She was an attractive girl, with soft, wavy brown hair, hazel eyes, fine features, and a disposition that combined gentleness and resilience.

Johnson's business proved as successful as his marraige. He quickly gained a reputation for good workmanship and honesty. In a day when the smallest circulating coin was the low-mintage and unpopular half-cent, many entries in Johnson's ledger reflected his precison with money. A piece of cotton lining cost 31¼ cents, a coat $5.36 ⅔, and an entry of 9 ¾cents represented "cash and tobacco." His going rates in the period 1829–32 ranged from $1.50 for making a vest or pair of pants to $10 for a complete suit, though barter was also common. Before long Johnson began taking in journeymen tailors himself, and some of these also boarded in his home for $1.50 per week. During the 1830s he acquired several pieces of town property, including a brick dwelling to replace the two-room frame structure that had been both shop and home and a hundred-acre farm outside of town for his mother and stepfather. Eventually he became prosperous enough to rent out some property and to make small loans to friends, which often went unpaid.

Johnson continued his self-education in his living room, on the nearby campuses of Greeneville and Tusculum Colleges, and in his tailor shop. Eliza was an accomplished and intelligent girl, and she set about teaching him to write and cipher. No wife could have given a more willing husband a more precious gift. His handwriting was labored, but with developing skill it took on a more open if still irregular quality, and the signature acquired a little flourish beneath, as if to signify pride of accomplishment. Difficult words like *communicate, together,* and *unbosom* often came through the spelling process unscathed, while easy ones like *come, get,* and *both* got blundered: *cum, git,* and *boath.* Over the years his writing improved, and although it was never free of blemishes, meaning was clear even where mechanics failed. Then again, high station and correct writing habits were not always matching characteristics in the nineteenth century.

The two colleges had debating clubs, and Johnson enjoyed going to meetings. One of his campus acquaintances observed many years later: "I well remember his fascinating manners, his natural talent for oratory, his capacity to draw the students around him, and make all of them his warm friends." Acquaintances, many, but warm friends of any duration, few. Throughout his life he was a very reserved about intimate friendships, and of all the people with whom he associated on the campus only one became a lifelong friend and adviser. That was Sam Milligan, a graduate of William and Mary, a teacher since the age of sixteen, and a sometime lawyer. He had a keen mind and a sympathetic, civilized approach to matters, and he appreciated Johnson's youthful spirit and dedication. Long after others had fallen by the wayside, Milligan remained as a trusted political and legal confidant.

Topics for debate often reflected the important political issues of the day and gave Johnson the opportunity to sharpen his interest in government. This was an era when young men could still be conscious of the nation forming around them, and there were many open questions of political wisdom and constitutional right. Andrew Jackson, hero of New Orleans and master of the Hermitage, near Nashville, had just come to the presidency; John Marshall held sway in the Supreme Court; Daniel Webster was just beginning his long career in the Senate; Henry Clay, "Gallant Harry of the West," would soon return to an interrupted career in Congress; and John C. Calhoun, momentarily buried in the vice-presidency, would soon surface as a spokesman when his beloved South Carolina decried the oppression of federal tariff policy.

Just as Selby had the services of a reader in his Raleigh shop, so Johnson paid a schoolboy to read in his own place of business. The selections ran heavily to the political, and since they were drawn from newspapers as well as college library books, the tailor shop became a clearing house for state and national goings-on. The college students often came in during their spare time to resume debates, and the commingling of students and artisans gave the shop a bustle that easily advertised it as the best source of an hour's fun. In his later political speeches Johnson showed that he cherished (and perhaps overdramatized) the tailor shop years, and he often employed a tailor's figure of speech to warn that the Constitution, like a pair of pants, could not stretch to fit what it was not designed to cover.

The townsmen attracted to Johnson's shop were a motley crew, including a tanner, a shoemaker, several farmers, and a lawyer. Chief among them, for his long-standing centrality in Johnson's life, was Blackston McDannel, the town plasterer. Three years younger than Johnson, "Old Mack" became a private sounding board, as Sam Milligan was a political one, and of all Johnson's letters during his public career the most personal were those to McDannel. These two men shared a mutual trust and understanding that in Johnson's life was a vote of confidence rarely given, for the tailor's early misfortunes had made him suspicious, distrustful, and introspective. Though McDannel's own personality was different, Johnson found in him a kindred spirit that he long cherished. McDannel, better than anyone else in Greeneville, understood his friend's personality and character—a challenge, indeed, that few people in Johnson's life could master.

The artisans and craftsmen of Greeneville, lumped together under the general term *mechanics,* formed a particular social and economic class, as they did elsewhere in the state. The average mechanic might earn as much as $500 per year, which approximated the wages of a clerk or a plantation overseer; unskilled labor, by contrast, drew $10 per month, and slaves were hired out for about $100 a year. Mechanics could thus be self-sufficient but not a great deal more, and their social ranking was very low. In the accepted scheme of things, laborers occupied a position lower than that of the poorest farmer even though they performed needful services.

Nor did working men participate in the affairs of government. The original state constitution of 1796, still in force, required that the governor possess a 500 acre estate, and members of the assembly 200 acres of land in the county they represented. Voting requirements were more complex. In addition to being twenty-one and male, a voter had to possess a freehold, a piece of land of unspecified value that he was legally capable of handing down to his heirs. However, this requirement could be waived if the person had lived in the county for six months previous to the election. Certainly by 1831 and perhaps earlier Andrew Johnson, at least, of the tailor shop crowd, met the freehold provision in its most restrictive interpretation. Regardless of how the law was worded, however, in practice few mechanics voted in state elections.

Discussions in the tailor shop regularly turned to local politics, and to the attitude of the local gentry. For there was indeed an aristocracy, even in a quiet little mill town like Greeneville. Men of this class, including one prominent landowner and the district's Whig congressman, had always run the affairs of Greeneville, and mechanics had customarily not sought the mayoralty or seats on the board of aldermen. Partisan warfare was not the issue, for Johnson's party affiliation did not become firm until 1840; nor was it even a matter of the mechanics seeing themselves the victims of wicked municipal ordinances. It really came down to a sense of propriety. Johnson and his friends with their few possessions were just as good, virtuous, and competent as the gentry with their many, and they could see no reason for a monopoly on the instruments of power.

Accordingly, in the spring elections of 1829 the mechanics set on foot a campaign to capture several positions on the seven-man board of aldermen, and of their slate not only tailor Johnson but plasterer McDannel and tanner Mordecai Lincoln won. Johnson came in last of the three, but in spite of his squeaky victory he gave good satisfaction and attended to little official things like street repairs and annual local poll tax rates with as much fidelity as he did to making Henderson a $2.50 "half-coat" or McKinnon a $6.66 suit. He enjoyed reelection in succeeding years, and in 1834 he became mayor. Yet Johnson's early political ventures did not mean a sudden and total break with the local gentry. He sought support among them and found some tolerance. Even those who resented the way he turned a political argument still liked the way he turned a hem.

The Johnson's family life during the 1830s also progressed harmoniously. In October 1828, a year and a half after the marriage, Martha was born in the back room of their first house. Early in 1830 came their first son, Charles, followed at intervals of approximately two years by Mary and Robert. As the children grew, they developed very differently. Martha had her father's solemn demeanor and dark complexion, while Mary was light skinned and light hearted and the boys outgoing and spirited. The family was clearly a patriarchal one in which the father, watchful and stern but reasonable and patient, was as attentive to the needs of his dependents as to affairs of business and politics. Yet politics he did not bring home; his tailor shop friends might cross his threshold as friends but not in any other capacity.

In addition to providing Johnson with a social and economic start in life and a position from which he could dabble at political issues the Greeneville years developed many facets of

Johnson's character. Most important was the conviction that hard work would overcome adversity and that people ought to do things for themselves. The irascibility and personal vituperation of his later years was not so evident, perhaps because his contacts were generally people of like mind who did not challenge or threaten him.

By the spring of 1835 Johnson had brought good fortune to himself by his own efforts. He had so far rectified the abuses of his childhood that no one could again look upon him as a man of little consequence or character, though the scars of those early years would never fully heal. Honors of various sorts had come to him, not alone political but educational as well; in 1832 the county court appointed the self-educated tailor a trustee of Rhea Academy, a position he cherished for years.

Johnson had every reason to be proud and content. With the people of east Tennessee he had a great affinity, for he and they were kindred spirits, with similar origins and harmonious values. Greeneville had a way of enticing men like Johnson to stay and find their happiness there. He would stay, and he did find happiness, but he was not content. A desire to serve his people and a need to fulfill himself, blending within him in an ambitious chemistry, drew his thoughts toward the state legislature.

I I

225 Miles on
Affairs of State
1835–1842

INDIAN SUMMER of 1835 came gradually to Nashville. "The Town," as middle Tennesseans called it with affectionate reverence, had progressed from its beginnings in the bitter winter of 1779 as a fortified compound where the Chickasaw Trail crossed the Cumberland River to a pleasant cultural center. By 1833 over $4 million in middle Tennessee cotton and other products left its docks. Imports that year exceeded $3 million and brought everything a plantation family could want, from anchovies and gold ear bobs to French cambrics and English steel. Country folk sold their produce at the market in the public square, which was open from dawn till noon on Tuesdays, Thursdays, and Saturdays.

The state legislature held biennial sessions beginning in October of odd-numbered years, and now, in the last days of September 1835, twenty-five senators and seventy-five representatives began to gather. As they arrived, the Nashville *Union,* one of several papers, told them what was going on in town. An outbreak of smallpox had largely subsided, but doctors still exhorted people to be vaccinated. The seventy-odd students of the University of Nashville faced their own scourge: annual examinations — freshmen struggled manfully with Xenophon and sophomores with Cicero, to say nothing of texts in math and science. John L. Brown, manager of the Union Street Lottery, announced over 3,000 prizes ranging from $4 to $5,000.

Andrew Johnson arrived at Nashville with his new colleagues, having traveled farther than all of them save one, who came from even deeper in the mountain valleys of East Tennessee. Everyone had been freshly elected, for two-year terms guaranteed a popular review of both houses after each regular session. The electoral process, very rudimentary by twentieth-century standards, had suited Tennesseans just fine for forty years. Politics here was an intensely personal business, without campaign committees or fund-raising drives. Reputation and personal following were paramount, and the loose factions that surrounded prominent figures had not yet promoted themselves to the status of parties in the national sense. A fellow simply tossed his hat into the ring, and that was that.

In the summer of 1835 Johnson declared his candidacy for the seat shared by Greene and Washington counties in the lower house. Washington did not know Johnson at all. Worse yet, it was the home territory of his well-regarded opponent, Major Matthew Stephenson. However, Johnson's personality and style suited the traditional method of campaigning. Candidates appeared jointly at important locations throughout the district, and the promise of political "speechifyin'" brought people for miles around from their isolated farms to meet friends, have some refreshment, and cheer as their favorite raked the opposition up one side and down the other. People sat by the hour for a good show, and Johnson quickly convinced them he was center ring. Five foot ten and about 175 pounds, at twenty-six he was developing a commanding physical presence. Those who knew him spoke later of his strong and resonant voice and his demeanor on the stump, which inspired confidence that he knew what he was talking about and cared what his listeners thought. Oliver P. Temple, who grudgingly respected Johnson and would later lose a close congressional race to him, observed that people always "went home believing that Andrew Johnson had told the truth."

In the 1830s state power was primary and federal power secondary. The state attended to the everyday wants and needs of its citizens; the federal government, more distant, performed limited functions of national importance. Congress possessed the constitutional power to tax, spend, and regulate interstate commerce. But the states, which had surrendered those powers in 1789, still played the watchdog, worrying about the constitutionality of specific measures. State legislatures elected national senators (the Seventeenth Amendment being eighty years in the future) and often sought to instruct them how to vote.

The two national parties, Whig and Democratic, held opposite views of the proper uses of constitutional power. The Whigs, led by Henry Clay and following the heritage of Alexander Hamilton, favored internal improvements such as roads, railroads, and canals at government expense, a high tariff to protect American manufactures, and a national bank chartered by Congress. This highly nationalistic economic program seemed to their opponents to benefit chiefly the wealthy and raised serious concerns about the proper function of the federal government. The Democrats, led by Jackson and following in part the Jeffersonian heritage, favored more limited federal economic functions so that the government would spend and take in less. However, in 1832 Jackson departed from a states rights philosophy to deny vigorously the constitutionality of South Carolina's attempt at nullification of the tariff.

Party labels did not mean much in Tennessee in 1835, but the voters soon understood who was who. Stephenson supported all of Clay's Whig economic programs. Johnson disclaimed official party affiliation but let it be known he liked the way Old Hickory had thrashed the nullifiers and battled the odious national bank, and independent farmers needed no high tariffs to protect far-off northern industries. And here appeared a leitmotif of Johnson's politics: the pride of his corps, the worth and dignity of mechanics and yeomen.

Election day was August 6, and when the votes were in, Johnson had thumped his opponent by 1,413 votes against 800. While he may have drawn some support from middle-class property owners in the towns, if not from the most wealthy aristocrats, most of his votes came from farmers and mechanics, and he would ever identify them as the bedrock of his political support.

This was an exciting time in Tennessee politics. The state had just given itself a new constitution. In the 1820s and 1830s popular aspirations for power and a general spirit of reform led to a good deal of constitutional carpentry in many states. Stymied for years in the Tennessee legislature, in 1833 the revisionists succeeded—Johnson often reminded people how he had signed one of the local calls for action—and a convention had liberalized requirements for voting, taxed land according to its value rather than at a fixed rate, abolished imprisonment for debt, and let the people rather than justices of the peace choose county officials. Some provisions required specific legislative implementation, and Johnson's was the first session to convene under the new frame of government.

Changing political leadership, both state and national, added to the hubbub. From 1839 until 1857, Democrats and Whigs were so closely balanced that only one Democrat, Andrew Johnson, served two consecutive terms as governor. Jackson's control in his own state also deteriorated. Loyally Democratic for twenty years, Tennessee's leaders possessed more ambition than the President knew how to reward, and in local contests he compiled a notorious record of backing the wrong candidate. Jackson's determination to have New Yorker Martin Van Buren as his successor in 1836 rather than home-grown Hugh Lawson White transformed some erstwhile Jacksonians into Whigs. For the rest of Jackson's lifetime—indeed, until 1856, during Johnson's governorship—Tennessee supported all the Whig presidential hopefuls.

The state found itself awash in the waves of a number of

national issues. Distribution to the states of the surplus treasury funds generated from sale of federal public lands presented questions both philosophical and practical; might not such distribution give the federal government a potent fiscal lever against the states? Banks presented no end of problems, particularly after the panic of 1837 ended their ability to redeem paper currency in specie, and financial stability eluded both the landed class and the lower economic orders. Even without federal funds, internal improvements grew apace, as states underwrote dubious ventures.

To attend to such grave matters, as well as the comparative trivialities of license waivers, fish dams, and divorces, Andrew Johnson came to Nashville. The legislature convened on Monday morning, October 5, 1835. Almost at once two highly political subjects of both immediate and long-range significance arose. In the choice of a United States senator Hugh Lawson White won unanimous reelection by the traditional method of a joint convention of both houses, in which each of the 100 members had one vote. Although Johnson did not object at the moment, before his final legislative term ended he would have a great deal to say on the convention method and would be a spokesman for change long before his own troubles with the Senate during Reconstruction.

A more divisive subject was the famous "Expunging Resolution." In the wake of Jackson's determination to cripple the United States Bank by removing its federal deposits the Whigs got up a furious storm, and Henry Clay introduced a resolution of censure in the federal Senate. Passed on March 28, 1834, it accused Jackson of "assuming upon himself authority and power not conferred by the Constitution and laws, but in derogation of both." Thomas Hart Benton, Jacksonian leader in the Senate, introduced a resolution to expunge the censure from the Senate journal. More than a simple repeal, expungement was a ceremony, the excommunication of an idea, so to say, in which the clerk of the Senate drew black lines through the original resolution and appropriately annotated the margins of the journal. By a 2 to 1 margin the Tennessee chamber tabled a resolution favoring expungement and instructing the Tennessee senators to vote for it. Johnson voted with the majority. It was an ironic issue to open the career of a man whose presidency would culminate in much more than a resolution of censure.

Shortly the House faced the main event of Tennessee's political circus: White as a presidential candidate. In 1833 he had shied away from the idea, but then Jackson rashly swore that if White "dared to become a candidate for the Presidency he would make him odious to society." Tennesseeans, peeved, could not see anything wrong with another favorite son following Old Hickory in the Executive Mansion. The popular and respected White certainly looked better than Van Buren, whose ties with northeastern labor and artisan shopkeepers, among other things, made cotton planters skittish. The Tennessee House of Representatives endorsed White's candidacy, 60 to 12, a quiet Johnson in the majority.

Thoughout these political maneuverings, indeed throughout his first term, Johnson maintained a low profile. He was hard-working, always present, and seldom voted for adjournments. Speeches were not officially recorded and published, and since the newspapers gave him little if any space, we can judge him only on the pattern of his votes. He intermittently presented routine petitions on local matters of concern to his district. He introduced only one minor bill, which made no headway, and enjoyed a few little successes with amendments to some administrative measures.

Of Johnson's few committee assignments the most sensitive was a select committee to consider how "to prevent the circulation, in this State, of seditious publications, and to protect the citizens thereof against the devices of certain evil disposed and misguided persons." The persons here stigmatized were the abolitionists, who delighted in plying planters, and sometimes even free Negroes and slaves, with unsolicited pamphlets and circulars. Outraged planters, still queasy with memories of Nat Turner's Virginia slave revolt, regarded this practice as a deliberate effort to foment insurrection. So widespread were the complaints that President Jackson would shortly propose a federal postal censorship law, thus igniting a sharp constitutional debate.

Tennessee, like other southern states, harshly proscribed the writing or circulating of any material "calculated to excite discontent, insurrection, or rebellion amongst the slaves or free persons of color" or the direct personal incitement of slaves or free blacks to "insubordination, insurrection, or rebellion." The bill passed, 38 to 34. Johnson opposed it, as did half the east Tennessee representatives. The reasons for Johnson's opposition are not certain. Clearly he was not an abolitionist, though when he later ran for governor, his opponents made that charge. He may have found a constitutional objection, for section nineteen of Tennessee's Declaration of Rights allowed every citizen to "freely speak, write, and print on any subject, being responsible for the abuse of that liberty." The explanation might also be geographical, for in east Tennessee slaves accounted for only about one-twelfth of the population, and the fear of slave revolts was not as high as elsewhere. Indeed, slavery was not a frequent subject of action during Johnson's years in the legislature. However, to circumscribe the Negro as a potential business competitor, he and fourteen of the easterners aided in the 55 to 11 passage of a law prohibiting free blacks from keeping any "grocery, tippling house, booth, or stall, for the purpose of vending spirituous liquors or groceries" on pain of a $50 fine. This law illustrates well how even a commitment to the principles of Jacksonian democracy did not moderate the belief of nonslaveholding white southerners, of whatever social and economic station in life, that blacks should have fewer rights and opportunities than themselves. Nor was the attitude peculiarly southern, as the record of discrimination in the North made evident. Johnson carried these views throughout his life, though they formed only one element of the philosophy of a highly complex individual.

The new state constitution, reflecting the current boom in internal improvements, "encouraged" the legislature to approve a "well-regulated system" thereof. In response, a spate of bills offered state assistance to a number of railroad schemes, some already under way, some generally aligned by surveys, and others merely envisioned by those who saw the glint of sunlight on iron in the neighborhood. The state would subscribe for a specified amount of the capital stock of each company, paying for it by the issue of twenty-five-year, 5 and ¼ percent state bonds. The stock dividends would presumably generate enough money to pay off the bonds when due, without levying taxes. A mortgage on the future it was, with a bottom line of $3,650,000.

Strategic Tennessee, and the isolated east in particular, needed railroads so that, as the committee report put it, "The beautiful streams, which burst forth from the hills and mountains, would exhibit, on every hand, the progress of the manufacturing and mechanic arts." But Andrew Johnson would have none of it. Railroads created unconstitutional monopolies, impoverished wayside tavern keepers, put wagoners out of work, and (according to his critics) scarred the beauty of nature by "pulling down hills and filling up hollows." He opposed the major bill and also subsidiary bills to charter the particular lines, whether sensible trunk routes or meandering milk run branches. He consistently opposed overspending, as well as alterations in the economic profile of east Tennessee by manufacturing or exporting. The East stood solidly in favor of railroads; on the major bill only three of the twenty-four east Tennesseeans, including Johnson, voted no, and his action contributed to his defeat at the next election. Yet Johnson did not oppose all internal improvements. Acts chartering turnpike companies or authorizing river improvements, even for distant parts of the state, received his approval as long as they did not drain state funds.

The total legislative output of Johnson's first session consisted of 91 public laws, 31 joint resolutions, and 140 acts of a private nature. Not all measures involved a roll call on final passage, but of those that did, half incurred Johnson's opposition; excessive spending, or bureaucratic proliferation, characterized many of them. Yet Johnson often had company in his naysaying. On thirty-five final roll calls, covering a wide variety of topics, Johnson's vote agreed with that of the east Tennessee majority on twenty-one occasions.

The legislature finally adjourned with a public dinner and Washington's birthday ball after a session of 141 increasingly stormy days. Johnson left for home with cash in his pocket and things on his mind. At $4 a day (the price of a middling coat) his salary came to $564, plus $88 for the 450 mile round trip. Perhaps, however, he esteemed more the education and the experience in moving from village mayor to state legislator. The issues were greater, the people more experienced and confident, the dangers of misstep more prominent. Ultimately it would be for the people to judge how well he had served their interests. But not quite yet. In October 1836 the Twenty-first General Assembly met once more in a three-week special session. The federal Distribution Act of June 1836 had assigned about $2 million of the surplus revenue to Tennessee. The legislature deposited the funds in three banks; Johnson wanted the money parceled out to the counties for the support of common schools. For the moment his idea failed, but in 1838 part of the interest did go to benefit education.

After Johnson returned to Greeneville, he had time to take stock of his position. In the presidential canvass of 1836 his man, White, carried Tennessee by nearly 10,000 votes, although he ran a poor third in the national electoral count. More important, since Greene and Washington counties went for Van Buren, Johnson wound up in opposition to his own constituents. In his earliest extensive letter on political matters, written on Christmas to George Washington Jones, a fellow legislator and one of his few close friends, Johnson considered even the questionable Van Buren preferable to an election by the House, as had happened in 1824. A constitutional amendment, he thought, should entrust presidential elections directly to the people, an idea he would later pursue.

Uppermost in Johnson's mind was his own reelection the following summer. Citing "pecuniary matters," he expressed doubt whether he would run again. "All to gether My family is young just coming up & I must try & save something for a rainy day—and if I keep dabling in politicks I shall loose my business & spend what little I have all ready made—" These concerns reflected inherent financial caution rather than imminent bankruptcy. Legislative duties occupied the members only for about five months every two years, and Johnson's business did not suffer. He employed several assistants and continued to deal in real estate in a small way.

Johnson rambled on: "My friends are sanguine of success if I run again, I donte like to be ta[u]nted too much by my enemies. I would rather die in the last dich than to be scared off the track; but if let alone I will retire for the present, the great object will be my defeet the next canvass, believing if I ame defeated I will be out of the way here after." He ran and lost, due in part to his opposition to railroads and his support for White, but the defeat, the first of only two he ever suffered in popular elections, hardly ended his career. With the help of popular disillusionment over east Tennessee's failure to benefit from the legislature's grand design for railroads, Johnson won back his seat in 1839.

Johnson's second term differed considerably from his first. Party lines had sharpened; two key roll calls, one to elect a United States senator and the other nominating presidential candidates for 1840, showed that forty-two Democrats faced thirty-three Whigs. The panic of 1837 and the aftermath of Andrew Jackson's unenlightened handling of public finance gave fiscal matters a particular urgency. In the spring of 1837 many state banks suspended specie payments, which left the country flooded with paper money that could no longer be redeemed in gold or silver. The value of such notes rapidly fell, and states had to decide whether, and how, to force banks to resume redemption. In Tennessee in 1839 the Democrats largely opposed resumption, and the Whigs favored it, for planter and business interests, involved in the interstate sale of cotton, required a stable currency and trustworthy banking facilities. The real question was the detail of how and when to resume, however, and after an erratic voting pattern Johnson finally joined in the passage of a resolution requiring all banks to redeem their obligation in specie as they became due and if they were presented for payment.

Small-denomination paper money seemed to offer a solution to the scarcity of small change, though it would exacerbate the problems of an unconvertible currency. To alleviate a burden on the poor, Johnson favored a bill to let the Bank of Tennessee issue notes of less than $5, but the House indefinitely postponed the measure. His general attitude on financial issues was one of cautious skepticism rather than deep hostility, a reluctant recognition that some banks were necessary, and a desire to keep state involvement at a minimum. Typical of his continued interest in the common man was his support of a truth-in-packaging law whereby purchasers of small quantities of salt and sugar, in premeasured sacks and barrels, who later found they had been short-weighted could sue the merchant and recover a dime a pound in damages.

The 1839 legislature took quite a cautious approach to internal improvements. The earlier grandiose plans for railroads having fizzled, macadam turnpikes now won approval, but bills creating specific companies prohibited state stock purchases, and they usually carried a saving clause permitting the state to alter or annul the charter whenever the public interest might demand it. This practice won favor in many states following John Marshall's 1819 decision in the Dartmouth College case, and such clauses improved the chances that Johnson would support turnpike legislation.

In this session Johnson began to show the tendency toward personal attack that later marred his career. When the Nashville *Whig* scoffed at the legislature and called it a gang of "Loco-Focos" (a term of derision referring to the most extreme antibank and antimonopoly faction of the Democrats), Johnson took the floor, bowed briefly in the direction of freedom of the press, and then jeered that "nature and phrenology had palpably marked" the editor as an "insidious being. . . .

He must have sir the feelings of a scavenger, a kitchen skullion, a reptile — a disgrace to his State."

Party lines shaped two familiar political issues, the election of United States senators and their instructions. As of October 1839 both senators were Whigs, White having converted following his break with Jackson over the presidency. For three days and forty roll calls, with the assistance of an earlier rule change introduced by Johnson, the Democrats held fast against Whig amendments to the instructing resolutions. In final form they required the two Whigs to support a whole list of Democratic positions: oppose a new national bank; support Van Buren's Independent Subtreasury bill; oppose a pending bill "to prevent the interference of certain Federal officers in elections," denounced as a violation of the First Amendment; oppose distribution of the proceeds from public lands and support instead a reduction of the price; support repeal of duties on imported salt; and "support, in good faith, the leading measures and policy brought forward and advocated by the present President of the United States, and to use all fair and proper exertions to carry out, sustain, and accomplish the same." Johnson consistently voted the party line. Rather than comply, both senators resigned six weeks apart, and the legislature replaced them with Democrats. The legislature also tried its hand at steering the next year's presidential bandwagon with a mid-October nomination of Van Buren and Governor James K. Polk for the 1840 Democratic ticket. Three years earlier Andrew Johnson rated Van Buren his second choice; if he still had reservations, he failed to vote them. Johnson's record during his second tour of duty had elements of both party regularity and independence. On political issues with direct national bearing his vote was safe. On state matters such as fiscal policy he deviated as he pondered the proper economic functions of government. He did not even always agree with Jacob Feazel, the other Greene County Democrat.

Johnson went home to Greeneville when the session ended in February 1840. Any doubts about his party alignment vanished when he announced a county-wide Democratic rally in town. Country folk poured in by the hundreds. Oliver P. Temple, an eyewitness and a Whig, testified to Johnson's smashing success in cementing a permanent and emotional popular alliance. First, a local official read a series of resolutions Johnson had written. They marshaled the greats of American politics back to the generation of the founding fathers into the forces of light and the legions of darkness, and Johnson then picked up himself where history left off. For almost three hours he praised Old Hickory and abused the Whigs. Clear, well-organized, articulate, and vigorous, but without ranting and raving, the speech had emotional appeal. As Temple said, "He took them as babes, and first by milk, and afterwards by strong meats, nurtured them into the stalwarts they became. He made of them a muscular race of men. He knew how to build men as well as how to clothe them . . ." Hill country Democrats, for whom Andrew Jackson had once been the pole star, now happily and confidently took their bearing from Andrew Johnson.

State Democratic leaders recognized Johnson's popular stature and named him an elector at large for the 1840 presidential contest in preference to a number of better-known figures. In this capacity he stumped the state, following a prominent Whig's itinerary a day or two later. He asked the editor of the Knoxville *Argus* to say "that the humble mechanic from old democratic Greene, like the youth of old, with his pebbles and his sling will be found at the western base of Walnutt Ridge, prepared for the combat." The "log cabin and hard cider" campaign of 1840 was particularly wild and woolly in Tennessee, and in spite of all that Johnson and the Democrats could do, Van Buren went down to defeat, with 48,289 Tennessee votes to Harrison's 60,391.

The results disheartened Johnson. "The truth is," he complained to Governor Polk in March 1841, "that we have too many in our ranks that is not willing to make any sacrifice for princable, but are under the entire controle of a sordid disposition." Polk had suggested that he run for Congress, but

Johnson demurred. "[I]t is very uncertain weather I take the field for any thing or not. my friends want me to run for the [state] Senat. what I shall do is uncertain. I intend to do all I can in or out of the canvass—" But summer always quickened the political blood in Tennessee. Johnson won the state senatorial seat from Greene and Hawkins counties, both safely Democratic, and thus joined a body of only twenty-five men. New ideas as well as revealing facets of his political character soon surfaced.

Due to the death of one incumbent and the expiration of the other's term, both federal Senate seats were now vacant. The Democrats had a majority of one in the Tennessee Senate, and the Whigs controlled the House by three, which meant that the joint convention method of election would produce two Whig senators. But the Senate Democrats, the "Immortal Thirteen," as the press dubbed them, boldly defeated the resolution to join the House in convention, thus preventing an election. The stalemate lasted the entire session.

In a long speech on October 27 and 28 Johnson defended the "Immortal Thirteen." After some paeans to Democratic heroes, a disquisition upon the word "faction," a snippet from *Macbeth,* and a stale French joke, he got to the main point and asserted that the Whig candidates would likely support measures harmful to the constitutional rights and best interests of the people, and thus he would violate his senatorial oath if he consented to their election. Furthermore, the convention method of election violated the federal Constitution, which required election to be by the "legislature"; nothing in either federal or state constitutions allowed conversion of the legislature into a convention. Each house, he averred, had to vote separately. Next came arithmetic, to show that the convention method, by merging the Senate vote in that of the House, disfranchised half the people of the state. He quoted the eminent jurist Chancellor Kent and declared that if need be, he had Story, Madison, Hamilton, and Jay in reserve. After praising the Constitution as "the Bible of our political faith . . . our cloud by day and our pillar of fire by night," he closed with some musings on the fact that the "immortals" numbered thirteen—just like the original states, stars, and stripes, he said, and (approximately) the "small band" who made a teapot of Boston harbor. And just like those gallant Spartans in the pass at Thermopylae, whose heroism won them bit parts in most nineteenth-century speeches on any side of all questions. "Leonidas fell but Greece was saved," he quoted from Herodotus, and went on to make sure everyone saw the parallel.

As a speech it was tolerable, as an argument weak, as partisanship transparent. It offered some inventive points, but the ultimate argument—"it is much better not to be represented at all than misrepresented"—left Tennessee without senators for two years. If this position was remarkable in a man who constantly affirmed representative government and had quietly sat in joint conventions before, yet Johnson became and remained for the rest of his life a consistent advocate of direct popular election of senators. Although the whole episode showed Johnson at his most partisan, the Immortal Thirteen did not cause a total breakdown of the legislative process because Whigs and Democrats did not always vote in solid blocs on general legislation, and on some significant measures the party lines got thoroughly fractured.

Because the regular session of 1841 had neither elected United States senators nor reapportioned the state legislature and congressional seats after the 1840 census, the governor, now Whig James C. "Lean Jimmy" Jones, called a special session for October 1842. The two hot political issues generated both stalemate and accommodation. On the election of senators the Immortal Thirteen stood together, and Tennessee went without senators until the 1843 Whig legislature chose two of their own. Apportionment of the state legislature brought out once more the personally vindictive side of Johnson. He believed that his home counties had been grossly abused. Large fractional excesses above the ratio had been ignored, with the result that Greene and Hawkins came out underrepresented while other counties were overrepresented. He charged that either "specious management" or "a want of political tact and sagacity, resulting from imbecility," or else "the result of a bargain and sale deliberately entered into" produced that outcome. He called one old enemy in the House a "political Judas," who had "brought seventeen hundred and seventy freemen into the market from the counties of Greene, Hawkins, Sullivan, and Washington, and sold them as sheep in the shambles, for *'the thirty pieces of silver.'* "

Johnson himself chaired the joint committee to apportion Tennessee's eleven congressional seats. The sensible solution was to arrange five Democratic and five Whig districts, leaving the eleventh at large. Proposed from the floor, with Johnson's support, this measure died, and the final lineup was six Whig and five Democratic districts. The easternmost district turned out to be safely Democratic, which gave the appearance of a neat little self-serving gerrymander by committee chairman Johnson. Actually, the district had reasonable dimensions; a middle Tennessee Whig proposed from the floor the alignment that finally passed; and Johnson voted against the bill.

Johnson did introduce into the apportionment debate an idea novel in Tennessee, though proposed in other states. He wanted legislative seats to be apportioned according to "the voting population, without any regard to three fifths of [the] negro population." He meant "slave population." The Constitution required Congress to apportion House seats among the states by "adding to the whole number of free persons, including those bound to service for a term of years, and excluding Indians not taxed, three-fifths of all other persons"—meaning slaves, not all blacks. But it did not require states to count three-fifths of the slaves in their own legislative apportionment. Johnson's proposal had nothing to do with attitudes toward blacks; he sought to increase the influence of east Tennessee at the expense of the middle and west with their large slave population. He lost, 3 to 22. Two days before final passage of the bill Johnson proposed a "general ticket" system, also novel in Tennessee but considered elsewhere, whereby each congressman would represent the district in which he lived but would be elected by voters statewide. Here a man who constantly championed localism was engaged in a last-ditch effort to prevent a Whig advantage in congressional seats. At that late date in the session a suspension of the rules was necessary, and the 13 to 12 party line vote fell short of the two-thirds mark.

"[I]f I were Pope I would give each of you a benediction," said Speaker Samuel Turney as he adjourned the Senate after its forty-five-day session. Johnson had not liked the special session at all—called "Lean Jimmy" 's message "the production of a diseased state of the human intellect"—and the only benedictions he needed were those of his constituents, for he certainly believed he had helped save the Democracy from at least some of the more dangerous Whig enormities. His career in the legislature, if somewhat checkered, traced his growth from a raw neophyte to a more reflective, visible state official. He had displayed some attitudes and addressed some issues that would become a central part of his life. He had made a few friends among his colleagues but could not claim statewide respect, and while he could rally his constituents behind him, he showed no ability to form and lead working coalitions in the legislature except for the limited partisan purposes of the Immortal Thirteen. He displayed none of the talents that would be necessary to avoid the pitfalls of his presidency. There were, however, indications, often indirect but sometimes clear, of a developing philosophy of the uses of constitutional power. His support for Democratic measures at the national level revealed a very limited view of the proper functions of government in economic matters, and even at the state level many of his votes carried only grudging assent. His seven-year record gave the farmers and mechanics of east Tennessee's green hills and valleys something to ponder. They did. And they concluded that Andrew Johnson was eminently qualified to be their national spokesman.

III

"Reiterate!
Reiterate! Reiterate!"

1843–1853

I THE 1840s the national capital was hardly a showplace. Drinking water offended the palate; sanitation facilities, the nose; and the streets, by seasons gooey quagmires and dusty swaths, conspired against foot, hoof, and carriage wheel. The public buildings, drafty and clammy, paled beside the stately edifices of Europe, and the capitol itself, like the Union unfinished, had a makeshift dome that resembled an upside-down wash basin. Ben: Perley Poore described the statues flanking the capitol's main doors: "War is represented by a stalwart gymnast with a profuse development of muscle and a benign expression of countenance, partially encased in ancient Roman armor, while Peace is a matronly dame, somewhat advanced in life and heavy in flesh, who carries an olive branch as if she desired to use it to keep off flies."

What Andrew Johnson, fresh from defeating by 543 votes his First Congressional District opponent, thought of these anatomical representations of the national destiny as in December 1843 he entered upon his first national office, we do not know. But before Johnson's ten-year career in the House advanced very far, two positions became quite apparent. He would regularly denounce appropriations for frivolous expenditures of all sorts. Peace might be a matronly dame, but she had better wear plain clothes. And he shared the robust nationalism, fearless of war and mindful of patriotic pride, that characterized the decade. For him the "stalwart gymnast" was the yeoman farmer and mechanic, well honed from contact with nature, springing to defend the country in time of need.

Ever the child of poverty and very sensitive to disparities of wealth, Johnson turned money issues into crusades. He strongly believed that limits on spending curtailed the government's ability to travel beyond narrowly defined constitutional functions or to become onerous to the common man. He regarded as frivolous the amassing of mementos of former presidents at government expense. The Smithsonian Institution, established in 1846, he thought useless but possibly worth salvaging if changed into a university "in the extended sense of the term," including manual labor, agriculture, horticulture, and other "mechanical subjects." Late in his service in the House he even proposed closing West Point and Annapolis. This represented quite a change of attitude, for he had often been solicitous on behalf of Tennessee lads seeking to be middies or plebes, and he had commented to Blackston McDannel in 1850 that he might like to have one of his own boys in the navy. Now, however, he complained that the army and navy were "the two great arteries by which this Government will be bled to death." He also objected to the selection process: "We see that lads who are blessed by nature with talents and with every requisite that would make them competent and efficient in the service are excluded, and that the sons of members of Congress, many of them almost imbecile, are crowded into these institutions."

The federal bureaucracy often raised Johnson's ire. Not only did he criticize the six-hour work day for government clerks, but he also accounted them a corps of smalltime Warwicks, who wrote mendacious political letters to the press after loitering around the city's hotels, faro banks, ten-pin alleys, and pistol galleries in search of gossipy tidbits. Make them work eight hours a day, he said; it would give them less time to make mischief and would be the equivalent, by his reckoning, of hiring 166 new clerks. He often proposed across-the-board pay cuts for federal employees whose salaries lacked constitutional protection, and when he once tried to get a pay raise for government workers "engaged in any branch of mechanics or at common labor," he lamented, "The man who wears the dinge of the shop or dust of the field upon his garments is never thought of or cared for by this House, except upon occasions when the Government needs taxes."

Johnson espoused a comprehensive financial program. A chief source of revenue was the tariff, and he agreed with the general southern position favoring the lowest rate possible. But the concerns of economic class rather than of sectional interest dominated his arguments. The rates, he insisted, must bear lightly upon workingmen and small farmers. When the chair found parliamentary fault with his motion to abolish all duties on salt and sugar, he retorted, "Just in answer to the Chair's decision, I will say that propositions to relieve the people from taxation never are in order."

A tariff for protection he found especially abhorrent, "a system of humbug," which allowed more profit to money invested in industry than in agriculture. He could find no constitutional warrant for a system that taxed one person for the benefit of another. During the debates that culminated in the Walker Tariff of 1846 he proposed a tax of 1 percent per annum on speculative wealth, including bank stock, government bonds and commercial paper, so that capitalists could no longer "live as drones in the hive, and feed upon the honey accumulated by the industrious bees." His ideas never made headway, but he pursued them at every opportunity.

In spite of Johnson's efforts at retrenchment he nonetheless did support the most expensive undertaking of the period. Manifest Destiny, combining self-righteousness and opportunity into a workable philosophy of national expansion, led adventuresome Americans into exciting but costly escapades.

On January 31, 1846, while relations with Britain over Oregon still threatened to become hostile, Johnson made his first major speech on foreign affairs. "Fifty-four forty or fight!"—the old Democratic slogan from 1844—was still his watchword. A fearless tone prevailed: "Why, the enemy may burn up a few towns, may sack a few cities, before we become entirely prepared; but the result will be that these outrages will tend to excite the patriotism of the country to a more determined and vigorous resistance."

America got neither fifty-four forty nor a fight, rather a logical compromise on Oregon, and national attention turned to the southern border. Johnson embraced the ultranationalistic position—Texas chose to enter the Union, the Rio Grande was the proper boundary, and Mexico was the aggressor. He shared the common disparagement of Mexicans as a "treacherous and perfidious race," and added: "The war ought to be prosecuted with sufficient energy, and for a suitable length of time, to make the Mexicans feel their own weakness and inability to cope with the American republic in arms, and their consequent dependence, so that they may hereafter be disposed to preserve religiously and scrupulously any treaties which they may make." Congressional critics of the war flirted with treason in urging early withdrawal from Mexico, he charged. "Are the American people, whose souls swell with animation and pride at the unfurling of their country's flag, who admire the majestic eagle's flight, and love to hear his screams of triumph and bold defiance, to take so humiliating and degrading a position as the one proposed by the opposition to the war?"

Johnson's full-scale support for the war aligned him strongly with President James K. Polk. The role of presidential defender was here an unaccustomed one for the man who rapidly lost defenders during his own stormy presidency. Indeed, with each of the four men who occupied the Executive Mansion during his tenure in the House, Johnson had at best tepid relations. For while Johnson had a limited view of the role of the federal government, he had an expansive, dynamic, Jacksonian view of the presidency as the head of both the executive branch and the party. For reasons both political and personal none of the four measured up to Johnson's expectations.

John Tyler did not satisfy Johnson on matters of patronage. Fellow Tennesseean and Democrat Polk, clearly the strongest executive between Jackson and Lincoln, knew Johnson from the factional labyrinth of state politics and thought him "vindictive and perverse in his temper and conduct." Nor did Johnson's vigorous support of the war and of Polk's vetoes improve his standing with Polk. On July 21, 1846, after having studiously avoided the President for some months, Johnson came to visit on some trivial matter and then engaged Polk in a full-scale review of their relationship. The President, rising easily to a well-accustomed state of high dudgeon, upbraided Johnson for "often finding fault" with the administration and for denouncing his appointment policies. The adjournment of this hour-long faceoff sent both men scurrying to their writing desks. Polk crabbed to his voluminous diary that even though he had lectured the tailor into a more submissive attitude, he would almost rather have a Whig in his place; Johnson fussed to friend McDannel, "He has a set of interested *parasites* about him—who flatter him till he does not know him self—He seems to be acting upon the principle of hanging an old friend for the purpose of making two new ones—"

Nor did Polk's departure in 1849 improve things. "Old Zachariah Taylor from what I can learn is a mad whig," Johnson had written in 1846 of the man who would succeed Polk, and Millard Fillmore gave him no greater pleasure. When his good friend William Lowry lost the Greeneville postmastership at the hands of Fillmore's postmaster general, he sighed, "You had better do as Cesar did in the roman Senate,—adjust your robe and fall as decent as possible—I would manifest no bad temper,—let them take it they will not have it long[.]"

Appointment policies that strained Johnson's relations with one president after another also led to a proposal for major reform. On January 13, 1846 he introduced by resolution a detailed scheme of rotation in office, designed to limit executive branch appointments to staggered eight-year terms, and to apportion federal offices by congressional districts. Later he would foreshadow the issue that would lead to his own impeachment by proposing that officials be removed only for "bad conduct." Johnson's resolutions at first got nowhere, but in typical fashion he kept trying. The *Globe* reporter paraphrased a statement in the spring of 1848: "Though Mr. J's attempts had again and again been given the go-by, yet he should proceed on the maxim of a great man, who has said 'Reiterate— reiterate—reiterate!' and as long as he should be able to lisp these principles of Democratic action, so long should he be found reiterating them here." He reiterated in vain until the last day of his service in March 1853.

Other major reforms enjoyed no more success. In 1851 and again the following year he proposed three constitutional amendments altering the electoral college system, requiring direct election of senators, and setting a twelve-year term for all federal judges, including Supreme Court justices. He had pondered the first two problems while in the state legislature. Specifically, he would now have state legislatures establish electoral districts to match the state's total number of senators and congressmen. The people would vote for president and vice-president on the first Thursday in August, and the candidate with the greatest number of votes in a district would thus earn one "electoral" vote. Absence of a majority of electoral votes would lead to a December runoff between the two leaders; a tie at the runoff would be broken in favor of the candidate with the greatest number of votes in the greatest number of states. This proposal was less radical than some made by others. The general democratic upsurge of twenty-five years had given rise to proposed changes of one sort or another, but a national constitutional tone of fundamental conservatism made the three branches resistant to structural tinkering.

In these efforts, as in his congressional career generally, Johnson perceived himself as a special protector of the people and never let slip an opportunity to expound upon that theme. Sometimes his fancies carried hin away, as in 1852, when it became apparent that a Whig legislature would gerrymander him out of Congress. Remembering passages from Matthew and Mark, he said of himself and a colleague: "Our political garments have been divided, and hereafter they will cast lots upon our vesture[.]" He was hardly a savior; neither was he a demagogue, though opponents often threw that charge at him. For a demagogue makes false promises as a way of gaining power for his own ends, and it could not be said of Johnson that he made promises he cared not to keep. None of his major legislative endeavors was empty rhetoric.

Johnson did everything an attentive congressman should do. He introduced routine petitions on all manner of subjects. Pensions for veterans and widows he pursued faithfully, even in such odd cases as that of a Tennesseean with several aliases who claimed that a cold suffered in the War of 1812 was now causing indigestion. The isolated settlements of east Tennessee hungered for political news, and enough of Johnson's letters survived the Civil War to show that he tried to be a conscientious correspondent. He could write a snappy, businesslike note to another government official, but his letters home contained an earthy honesty, wry humor, and informative observations on issues familiar to the recipient. "Friend Milligan," he began a few days after Christmas 1852, "I having just returned from tea, being all alone in my room and in a rather sombre mode, I concluded by way of relief to scrawl down a few incoherent lines to one it has always been a plasure to commune with whil in a view of this kind." There followed over three long pages of views about appointments under President-elect Pierce, the future of the party, the composition of the Cabinet, the weather, the illness of mutual friends, and other newsy items. Even though he frequently apologized for his literary shortcomings, his letters, if still roughhewn, presented no problems of comprehension.

A great deal of cynicism marked Johnson's observations of national politics. In February 1844 he lamented, "What our fate is to be as a party, God only knows, there is one thing, I am well assured of, that is we have no leader in the House of Representatives that is worth one cent. We are moving on pel-mel, without any particular object in view what ever—" In January 1847 he concluded a letter to McDannel, "I have no news of interest to give you, the democratic party is gone to hell no mistake—"

Nor did he like the principal presidential hopefuls, though Sam Houston of Texas and Lewis Cass of Michigan ranked high. For Stephen A. Douglas he reserved special scorn: "Douglas, the candidate of the *cormorants* of our party & Some few adjuncts from the other, is now considered a dead cock in the pit, unless Some throe in the agony of political death Should enable him to kill off his opponents which is not likely to occur—He is a mere hot bed production, a precocious politician wormed into, and kept in existence by a Set of interested plunders that would in the event of Success, disembowel the treasu[r]y, disgrace the country and damn the party to all eternity that brought them into power—"

Even with Douglas fallen by the wayside, the summer campaign season of 1852 left Johnson gloomy. The doings of the Democratic convention underscored his desire to abolish conventions as unrepresentative of popular will and replace them with direct election. He thought the Democratic platform, by approving the constitutionally dangerous Kentucky and Virginia Resolutions of 1798–99, gave southern "ultras" an advantage over southern Unionists and made it appear as though disunionists and nullifiers would enjoy an inside track with Franklin Pierce. Yet he dutifully stumped Tennessee for ex-Brigadier General Pierce and defended him from the oft-repeated charge that he had fainted from cowardice at Contreras in 1847. (Actually, the problem was a painful bruise embarrassingly low in the groin, suffered when his horse bolted and threw him forward against the pommel of his saddle.) Johnson thought no better of Pierce after the election and lamented in December, "I fear Pierce will prove him Self to be a mere Yankee after all—" He thought Pierce had become president too suddenly, without sufficient "political probation." The elevation of Washington and Jackson he called "destiny," that of Pierce "manufacture."

Every two years Johnson had to present his own record to the yeomen and mechanics at home, and in spite of his frequent protestations of humility he enjoyed the quest and exercise of power on their behalf. Occasionally he even admitted it in the House, noting that flattery "from men who wielded the scissors or the plough" was "most dear" to him.

Sometimes, however, his reelection proved difficult. In 1845 his opponent was "Parson" William G. Brownlow. Possessing not only a flamboyant self-righteousness and unlimited mendacity but his own newspaper as well, the parson had all the tools to abuse the tailor. Johnson called Brownlow a hyena, a devil, and a coward; retaliatory headlines branded Johnson "a vile calumniator, an infamous demagogue, a common and public liar, an impious infidel, and an unmitigated villain." To the charge that he had played cards on the Sabbath and then gone about the streets of Greeneville proclaiming that "Jesus Christ was a bastard and his mother a strumpet" Johnson replied that he believed in "the great scheme of salvation as founded, taught, and practiced by Jesus Christ himself." To the assertion that he was a bastard himself Johnson responded with documentation acquired on a special trip to Raleigh. After his victory Johnson observed: "The fact of a farmer or mechanic stepping out of the field or shop into an office of distinction and profit, is peculiarly offensive to an upstart, swelled headed, iron heeled, bobtailed aristocracy, who infest all our little towns and villages, who are too lazy and proud to work for a livlihood and are afraid to steal."

The ups and downs of his political career sometimes left Johnson depressed. One notable low point occurred in January 1847 when a combination of personal and political burdens seemed to converge. Knowing that he was out of favor with the administration, looking forward to the elections that summer, and believing that even some of his closest friends at home, including Sam Milligan, were coming to doubt his positions and principles, he poured out his heart to Blackston McDannel, always his last refuge in times of despair. "[T]he clouds look white and angry," he noted of a gloomy Sunday morning. A snowstorm, most likely, and appropriate, too, considering his view of politics—"the government Seems pushing on to destruction in Spite of all that can be said and done," —and his own health—"legs, arms, head, and heart all seem to have entered into a conspiracy against my peace and happiness." Some of his real-estate involvements in Greeneville were failing, but he seemed not to care, for Greeneville had now even lost all the qualities of home: "If I should hapen to die among the damned Spirits that infest Greeneville, my last request before death would be for some friend (if I had no friend which is highly probable) I would bequeath the last dollar to Some negro as pay to take my dirty Stinking carcas after death, out on some mountain peak and there leave it to be devoured by the vultures and wolves or make a fire Sufficien[t]ly large to consume the Smallest particle that it might pass off in Smoke and ride upon the wind in triumph over the *god for* saken and hell deserving mony loving, hypocritical, back bighting, sundy praying scondrels of the town of Greeneville— . . . Send me some new fangled oathes So that I can more effectually damn Some of that brood in and [about] the town—" Such depths of despair were most unusual, and even McDannel must have been a bit surprised.

But if such deep melancholy did not often bother him, Johnson was nonetheless unhappy in Washington. Like most congressmen, he left his family behind, and being an absentee father of four teenaged sons and daughters did not appeal to a family-oriented man. When Johnson did not hear from them regularly, he worried. "I think my family must all be dead for have not heard from any of them for 20 days—Write to me soon and give me all the news," he entreated David Patterson, later to become Martha's husband. On another occasion, receipt by the same mail of a good letter from each of his four children delighted him, and he responded to daughter Mary, "After your letter came I had one right harty laugh over some of your nonsense."

Johnson took pains to bring up his children properly, even from a distance. A fatherly letter advised Mary, at the time an eighteen-year old at the Rogersville Female Academy, to get in the habit of "writing a hand Some heavier than you do" and to prepare through education for a useful life. "Never mind the bacon and cabbage[.] there are ma[n]y human beings who think they are living sumptiously if they onely have plenty of good bacon and cabbage—"He wanted Mary to learn a lesson from the plight of a friend expelled for misbehavior. "In School sustain yourself as honorable and highminded—be guilty of no low and vulgar acts or expressions even with your associates, for there is the place to make a good character and to induce others to form a high opinion of you— ... To day persons are friendly to morrow they burst into as many pieces as touchmenot—The true policy is to be friendly with all and too friendly with none—"

The last bit of advice Johnson followed himself in Washington, and all his life, for that matter. During his first term he roomed at Mrs. Ballard's, one of the numerous boarding houses for congressmen on Capitol Hill, along with four other members. Later he moved to Mrs. Davis's on the north side of E Street between Ninth and Tenth, apparently by himself; in his last term he stayed at the well-patronized United States Hotel. But he always seemed isolated socially from the rest of the Tennesseeans as well as from the House at large. In the one surviving account of a night on the town he described an outing with two or three of "our old companions in arms" as "a Kinder of a 'bust,'—not a big '*drunk*.' " They took the train to Baltimore, had an oyster supper, and then went to a Viennese children's ballet, after which they rested "in perfect quiet" on their "virtuous couches" till the seven A.M. train to Washington. "And here I am now at 11 O'clock A.M.—neither sick drunk nor groggy, finishing my paper to my old well tried and faithful friend and pilcher 'Mack.' "

Normally correct and proper in official dealings with colleagues, Johnson nonetheless exchanged barbs with anyone, particularly if he detected a slur upon his working class. No less a figure than Jeff Davis once referred slightingly to tailors and for his temerity got called a representative of an "illegitimate, swaggering, bastard, scrub aristocracy." Johnson also accused the venerable John Quincy Adams of seeking to break up the Union by his persistent introduction of antislavery petitions, yet did the old man the kindness of selecting him a seat at the opening of the short session of the Twenty-ninth Congress, when Adams was too ill to attend, and offered it to him upon his return. Of Thomas L. Clingman, whose celebrated 1845 duel with firebrand William L. Yancey produced no wounds but prodigious fright, Johnson chuckled to McDannel, "Some persons are wagish enough, to insinuate, that he not only made a copeous discharge of water, but that his Short bread came from him in grat profusion—how true this is I will not undertake to Say—" The South Carolinians he thought "impudent" and the Alabamans "tinctured with disaffection, particularly a blather mouthed fellow by the name of Belser, that has a great deal more courage than good conduct—" But then, good conduct was never a notable characteristic of House proceedings in this period. Johnson usually sat in the fifth row and just off the center aisle, but so difficult was it to get recognized that in the course of five terms he made only twenty-five speeches of significant length, and regular shorter comments.

Johnson touched at one time or another upon almost all the current topics of national consequence. He also revealed an increasingly complex political profile. No longer was he the local politician of limited outlook whose public duties fostered a provincial approach. Johnson made the transition to national office at a significant time in his own life and in that of the nation. His generation of congressmen included many who, like him, would serve their chosen national causes in the coming conflict of arms. At one time or another his colleagues included Thaddeus Stevens, Jefferson Davis, Alexander H. Stephens, George W. Julian, Preston King, Horace Mann, Robert Barnwell Rhett, Horace Greeley, John C. Breckinridge, Hannibal Hamlin, and Sterling Price. Even his 1864 running mate was there for a brief time, though how much acquaintance they had beyond a casual chat about family history, remembered by Lincoln in 1854, is not known.

Johnson was a southerner at a time when the South became increasingly defensive about its way of life (in much of which he did not share) and correspondingly forward about its political privileges. He spoke for farmers and laborers at a time when his section, once in the forefront of democratic reform, seemed to drift back into aristocratic hegemony. Under Polk, whom he had otherwise sharply criticized, he defended a vigorous concept of the presidential veto, and thereby a strong executive, during the administration of the only strong executive between Jackson and Lincoln. He favored fiscal and constitutional conservatism in most federal legislation, both of which positions he carried to greater lengths than prevailing sentiment. He was a continentalist, a national expansionist, at a time when that popular philosophy, if implemented by his sectional confreres, might not produce what Jefferson had called an empire for liberty. Moreover, he favored Union at a time when some of his colleagues, denied their way, thought to break up the Union.

Nowhere did the views of Johnson and the fate of the nation more closely touch than in two concurrent subjects. The Homestead Bill, which Johnson introduced in March 1846 but which did not become law until 1862, offered the first workable plan for free distribution (rather than sale) of the federal public domain. The original version permitted any "poor man who is the head of a family" to enter 160 acres of public land "without money and without price" (for Johnson liked Isaiah 55:1), and to receive title to it after four years of residence and cultivation. Proof of poverty rested on the applicant's own affidavit, made to the local land office, that he was "destitute of means to purchase" a quarter section and the evidence of "three respectable House-holders" that the applicant was not only poor but "of good moral character."

This first effort made no headway, but Johnson, with characteristic determination, regularly reintroduced his bill. He also revealed a willingness to compromise or adjust details to save a basic principle—a talent unfortunately lacking in most of his presidency. In the version that the House finally passed in

1852 the requirement of poverty became a requirement simply that the applicant not own any land.

At first Johnson's bill seemed merely the project of a visionary agrarian, and a dangerous one at that. Railroad promoters saw it as a threat to subsidies. Land speculators moaned. Southerners, horrified, thought it an abolitionist measure designed to close off the West to slavery expansion by encouraging free farmers, especially when Horace Greeley began bannering the idea in his New York *Tribune*.

The Tennesseean shepherded his homestead project with more skill than his other legislative endeavors. Ever one for the "now, statistics prove" approach, he produced mountains of figures to buttress his arguments and was well known to the circulation clerks at the Library of Congress. He courted strange constituencies, like the high-tariff advocates, by asserting that prosperous, producing farmers would be better able to afford dutiable foreign luxuries—never mind that these plain, homespun men of nature were supposed not to want such things, anyway. He weaned some southern colleagues away from their original antipathy, and the final vote of 107 to 56 represented a broad intersectional coalition. For once Johnson could emphasize positive things. Many of his other enterprises put him so often in the position of naysayer that he must have seemed to his colleagues a grating, parsimonious scold. The pastoral qualities of homesteading, however, gave him opportunities to create a panorama on the canvas.

Johnson portrayed the homesteader as "a better citizen of the community. He becomes qualified to discharge the duties of a freeman. He comes to the ballot-box, and votes without the restraint or fear of some landlord. He is in fact the representative of his own homestead, and is a man, in the enlarged and proper sense of the term. After the interchange of opinions and the hurry and bustle of the election-day is over, he mounts his own steed and returns to his own domicile, where all of his cares and his affections centre. He then goes to his own hay mow, to his own barn, to his own corn-crib, to his own stable, and feeds his own stock. His wife, the partner of his bosom, on the other hand, turns out and milks their own cows, churns their own butter, and at the proper time, when their rural repast is ready, he and his wife, with their little fair-haired, white-headed ties of affection, sit down at the same table together to enjoy the sweet product of their own hands, with hearts thankful to God for having cast their lot in this country where the land is made free, under the protecting and fostering care of such a Government."

Manhood, independence, self-contained political power, possession of the earth and mastery over it, the Puritan work ethic, the sanctity of family, devotion to God and country— it was all there, a finely drawn intellectual and emotional self-portrait of pre-Civil War America. And, if one exchanges the tailor's scissors for the farmer's plow, of Johnson himself, for in all these things he believed and for all of them he had spoken.

On constitutional points Johnson began with the treaty power, which he believed gave the nation the right to acquire land for the purpose of "settlement and cultivation." The territorial clause in Article IV, Section 3, he said authorized Congress to pass laws to encourage settlement. He agreed that money collected from one part of the people could not be distributed to another but asserted that there was no bar to the distribution of land; therefore, the government could appropriate public lands "for some purposes embracing wider limits and greater range of objects" than it could with money. Here was a remarkable, almost twentieth-century concept of the federal government's power to "promote the general welfare" of the United States, which Johnson had casually mentioned as a proper object of spending. The general welfare clause was anathema to states' righters; yet by simply asserting that appropriating land differed from appropriating money, the general welfare could be furthered without leaving the states' righters much of a target. Well might John Marshall have smiled at such reasoning and tactics. Perhaps there was a bit of Hamilton in the whole case, too, for Johnson sought to tie the common man as a social and economic class to the federal government the way Hamilton had done with the rich.

The homestead fight made Johnson more of a national figure than any of his other projects. Greeley and other editors gave him increased space; labor conventions in the North invited him to speak and even proposed him as a presidential candidate. The struggle was long, however, and after the House finally passed the measure on May 12, 1852, it died in the Senate. Both houses later passed a similar measure when Johnson was a senator, but James Buchanan vetoed it. For Abraham Lincoln, the railsplitter, Johnson's counterpart in background, would be reserved the signing of the Tennessee tailor's favorite measure.

America's prewar acquisitiveness left a legacy of questions —not just how to populate the land but also how to organize it politically. Slavery and sectional power struggles lay at the heart of this dilemma. In 1820 a great sectional compromise had settled the fate of slavery in all the unorganized territory then under the flag, conceding to Congress the constitutional authority to close a large part of the national domain to slavery prior to statehood. But the subsequent annexation of Texas, Oregon, and the Mexican Cession reopened the issue. With increasing aggressiveness abolitionists demanded that Congress close all federal territories to slavery; southern extremists demanded positive federal protection for slavery. The long first session of the Thirty-first Congress, from December 1849 to September 1850, hammered out a solution. The measures originated in the Senate, and Johnson played only a nominal role in the House debates, but his attitude and votes reflected important principles.

Johnson had become a slaveowner himself just before entering the House. In 1842 he purchased a girl named Dolly, and then her half-brother, a thirteen-year-old named Sam whose bill of sale valued him at over $500. The census of 1850 listed four slaves, two adults and two children, who performed domestic chores in the household. This proprietary interest hardly made Johnson a prominent defender of the institution, however. Indeed, he seldom spoke on the subject. In his first term he defended the "gag rule" as an appropriate way of handling antislavery petitions. On January 31, 1844, while debating the proposed (and shortly accomplished) repeal of the rule, he attacked the "deliberate design on the part of some gentlemen to effect, if possible, a dissolution of the Union." Slave property enjoyed constitutional protection, he said, and he urged all southern congressmen to "come up on this question as a band of brothers, joining in one fraternal hug; heart responding to heart; turning their faces towards heaven, and swearing by their altars and their God, that they will all sink in the dust together before they will yield the great compromise contained in the constitution of their fathers." He was correct that several constitutional provisions recognized the existence of slavery and that the fugitive slave clause protected it. The question was, How far did congressional power over the subject extend?

Johnson shared the prevailing notion that blacks were inferior; he complained that a bill to incorporate the trans-Potomac town of Alexandria would, by expanding the franchise, "place every splay-footed, bandy-shanked, hump-backed, thick-lipped, flat-nosed, wooly-headed, ebon-colored negro in the country upon an equality with the poor white man." In April 1848 he asked whether Massachusetts Whig John Palfrey would want a daughter to marry the bright young black whom Palfrey had equated in ability with his own son; during a subsequent exchange of "personal explanations" Johnson averred he had not intended to insult Palfrey or his family.

Political concerns, however, dominated Johnson's thinking. A speech at Evans' Crossroads, not far from Greeneville, on May 26, 1849, had outlined his position. Slavery was now "one of the principal ingredients of our political and social system, or in other words, a part of the warp and the woof, and cannot be prematurely removed without spoiling the web." He regarded it as a political liability, since the Constitution's three-fifths clause allowed the South twelve less congressmen than they would have had if all slaves were free laborers. Lincoln's proposal for compensated emancipation in the District of Columbia he rejected because it made both owners and nonowners foot the bill. Nor could Congress close the territories to slavery. Johnson warned of impending disunion and urged everyone, regardless of section or party, to resolve "that we will stand by the Constitution of the country and all its compromises, as our only ark of safety, as the palladium of our civil and religious liberty, that we will cling to it as the mariner clings to the last plank, when night and tempest close around him."

As tempestuous scenes enveloped the House during the winter of 1849–50, it became obvious that the stumbling block to solution of national problems was California, whose admission would shift the balance in the Senate in favor of the free states. On March 13, 1850 Johnson suggested admitting California, recognizing territorial government in the rest of the Mexican Cession, strengthening the fugitive slave law, and returning the District of Columbia to Maryland. Except for the last provision, Henry Clay had introduced all of these proposals in the Senate in January.

On June 5 Johnson took the floor. "I am for the Union so long as it can be maintained without a violation of the Constitution," he said, "and I am prepared to go for a settlement, a reasonable settlement, of this question." Shortly he would have an opportunity to redeem his pledge. Between September 6 and 17 Clay's five measures from the Senate came to a vote in the House. First came the bill establishing New Mexico Territory and adjusting the Texas boundary, then statehood for California, then territorial status for Utah, then the strengthened fugitive slave law, and finally the abolition of the slave trade in the District of Columbia. Johnson approved the first four, which gave him a much better record for agreeableness than many southerners. Out of forty-four who voted on all five bills only three approved all of them, and six besides Johnson approved four. The California bill involved a matter of congressional discretion; the fugitive slave law strengthened what southerners long regarded as an absolute constitutional right; the Utah and New Mexico measures, by allowing territorial populations to decide the question of slavery, transferred the scene of argument without finally settling the question of congressional power.

"The brightest and best hopes of man"—thus had Andrew Johnson discerned the benefits of Union in August 1850. And the Union was saved, at least for a little while, at least until a Civil War in which his quiet erstwhile collegue would strive to save "the last, best hope of earth." The Compromise of 1850 allowed a great national release of tension, and it must have been an emotional high point of Johnson's service in the House. For sheer gratification, however, nothing could compare with the House's passage of the homestead bill, particularly because by the time it got through in the spring of 1852, Johnson knew that his service was drawing to a close. The state legislature that met in October 1851 belonged to the Whigs, and in redistricting the state, they gerrymandered him out of office—"Henrymandered," he always called it, a barb for Gustavus Henry, a leading Whig.

"So far as I am concerned I have no political future," he noted among some scribbles for future use in speeches, probably in the spring of 1852. Referring to his opponents, he mused, "I have bent my Speare upon their crests and they in turn have shiverd ma[n]y a lance upon me—" Twisting a bit the usual southern chivalric pretensions, he liked to think of himself as a poor man's knight, a champion of those who could not take the field for themselves. His voting pattern continued many themes from his prior Tennessee record—against spending, against bureaucracy, against dubious federal functions, against more than he was for, indeed. But for Texas, for Oregon, for the Mexican War, for protection of slavery, and, most personally, for homesteads.

In December 1852, as his last session of Congress got underway, Johnson acccounted himself a success, considering his deficiencies of education and wealth. Were he to leave public life then, he thought his record would place him "greatly above mediocrity as compared with politicians in the aggregate: a position, one So humble as I am ought to be satisfied with—"

Other things, too, might well have impelled him to be satisfied. He had fussed periodically about an unspecified ailment, and the illness that would gradually make his beloved Eliza an invalid began to appear. His two boys, Charles, twenty-two, and Robert, just out of his teens, faced a mixture of medical and personal problems. On top of that, Johnson had just become a father again. Andrew, Jr. (always to be called Frank), the last child, was born in 1852, eighteen years after Robert. Yet Johnson could never be satisfied. To David Patterson in December he readily admitted his ambition but added, "[I] have always been determined not to let it, run me into excesive error or cause me to aske too much at the hands of highly esteemd friends who had long been my constant and ardent Supporters." However, before December was out, Johnson eyed the governorship and hinted, "If there was a correspondence gotten up with some fine men in different parts of the State and have it understood that there was to be no convention and by general consent let the candidate who ever he may be have the track as the '*peoples candidate,*' it would be worth ma[n]y votes to the party—" The tailor could certainly mark out a pattern to fit his own cloth. And on the face of it, at least, it was not "excesive error." He won.

I V

A Rung on
Jacob's Ladder
1853–1857

ANDREW JOHNSON had made a middling congress-
man, always attentive to his constituents, persistent about his
principles, and partially successful with a few, though not
most, of his proposals. Among such men, some are frustrated
would-be executives. Johnson fit this mold. Fiscal reform, bureaucratic trimming, and electoral changes, if they were to
succeed, belonged in the legislative messages of an authorita-
tive, respected executive who possessed the institutional tools
to see a program through. Perhaps four years of executive
service in Nashville might be more fruitful than ten of legislative experience in Washington.

Yet few characteristics of the Tennessee governorship, con-
stitionally impotent since statehood in 1796, fit Andrew Johnson. The governor nominated very few officials. He shuffled
routine stacks of papers, none of them any more important
than individual pardons or processes for extradition. That
vague but expansive duty upon which an otherwise strong
executive could capitalize — to see that the laws were faithfully
executed — was in this case essentially unenforceable. The

permission to address messages to the General Assembly seemed more a polite token of official dignity than an invitation to vigorous leadership, for, possessing neither veto nor patronage, the governor could do little in a showdown with the other branch.

Most southern governorships of the 1850s labored under similar restraints. Legislative preeminence being long accepted, the governorships bestowed upon planter aristocrats a sort of elder-statesman dignity and commensurate social standing, or else they attracted ambitious men in their prime who sought a springboard to national office.

Johnson belonged in the latter group. In the spring of 1853 the Tennessee governorship offered a target of opportunity, in fact, about the only one. Redistricted out of a virtual sinecure, he could not move to the Senate because the seat to be filled in 1853 would likely remain in Whig hands, and the other would not come vacant until March 1857. Some friends believed that the homestead project might get him the vice-presidency, but the next opportunity was three years off, and he could hardly go directly from forced retirement to the national ticket. The governorship, if dull, at least presented an opportunity to mark time in the public view. Moreover, since the statehouse was the traditional property of middle and west Tennessee, to be the first eastern chief executive in over thirty years offered a bit of pleasure the parochially proud Johnson could well savor.

The nomination required skillful work, for Johnson was never as popular with the party brass as with the rank and file. The party leadership came mostly from middle Tennessee, and Johnson's deep distrust they fully reciprocated. Left to their own inclinations, they would never have chosen him, and so he amassed enough pledged or instructed delegates among the county organizations to force the convention to choose him.

The Whigs put up Gustavus Henry, of "Henrymander" notoriety, thus giving Johnson a ready-made issue and personal target. Together they canvassed the state all summer in the traditional way, making more than forty joint appearances. Two more opposite styles could hardly be found. Henry, the "Eagle Orator," reputed kin to the renowned Patrick, classmate of Jeff Davis at Transylvania University, discoursed with flowing eloquence; Johnson, the tailor's helper, kin to nobody of consequence, classmate of nobody at all, hammered away with facts and figures.

When Henry praised banks and tried to make points with the national Whig program of broad federal functions, Johnson recited the small-government Democratic litany. When Henry hinted darkly that Johnson's proposed constitutional amendments would reopen the slavery controversy and harm the South, Johnson called the argument "a mere bugaboo" and detailed the cumbersome nature of the Electoral College, the antirepublican character of lifetime judicial tenure, and the tendency of senators to "pamper and enrich personal and political favorites."

By the hour this sort of thing went on, and the crowds loved it despite the beastly hot and humid weather. Personal rudeness seldom intruded, but neither passed up an opportunity to put the other in his place. At Memphis, with its large Irish population, Henry made much of Johnson's 1847 vote against government-funded relief for the victims of Ireland's potato famine. Admitting the vote, Johnson reminded everyone that he had also urged congressmen to give on their own, produced from his pocket the receipt for a fifty-dollar donation, and asked his chagrined former colleague, "How much did you give, sir?" The audience howled—"prolonged and deafening applause," so the Memphis *Appeal* said, and the editor generally remarked upon the "close" logic and "clear, distinct, and engaging" character of Johnson's address. His margin of 2,250 out of nearly 125,000 votes was the largest in ten years and reflected the close balance of parties.

On inauguration day Johnson gave an address the likes of which Tennesseeans had never heard on such an occasion. He arraigned the Whigs for regarding the Constitution as "a paper wall, through which they could thrust their fingers at pleasure, or a piece of gum-elastic that could be expanded or contracted at the will and pleasure of the Legislature." Next he scored a social and economic aristocracy which, he said, totally failed to understand democracy. In his view, democracy and Christianity represented harmonious, converging branches of a movement to purify and elevate man both politically and spiritually. "Democracy progressive" and the "Church Militant" were both "fighting against error—one in the moral, the other in the political field." When they converged, the "Church Militant" would become the "Church Triumphant," and "Democracy progressive" would become "Theocracy." It was all quite simple, he said, like a political version of Jacob's ladder, which everyone could climb according to their worth. The "young men" ought to find rungs matching their virtue and merit and occupy them "with honor to themselves and advantage to their country."

After such a preachy detour—and they were in the McKendree Church, the new capitol being unfinished—anything else could only be anticlimactic. But Johnson rambled on a bit. Federal aid to internal improvement he seriously questioned; state aid, if within the economic ability of the people, could properly perfect a "judicious and well-regulated system." After the inevitable reminder about homesteads, a few stray kudos for Jefferson's famous 1801 comment about "entangling alliances," and a bit of grousing about military expenditures, he promised a later message on specific legislative proposals and thanked his auditors for their patience, by now doubtless worn thin.

Johnson's opponents hooted; his supporters cautiously kept as quiet as decency would allow and hoped for a sterling performance in the forthcoming legislative message. They enjoyed a measure of reward. Johnson, out of direct touch with local issues for ten years, prepared his "state of the state" message carefully, analyzing major problems in detail and suggesting specific remedies. Most of them, like his proposal to liquidate the state's capitalization of banks, reflected his fiscal conservatism and limited view of government. He also favored tax reform, road improvement, prison reform, and a simplified judicial structure. For education he urged full support, including a statewide tax. If Tennessee could afford a fancy new capitol, he asked, why not a proper system of elementary schools?

The marked contrast between his legislative message and his inaugural epistle in the McKendree Church illustrates the dimensions of Johnson's personality. The inauguration marked a personal triumph for Johnson and a symbolic triumph for the democracy's rank and file, whom he believed he embodied. On such occasions rhetorical restraint did not appeal to the Greeneville tailor, but if the inaugural was self-indulgent, the legislative message was intelligently functional. Emphasizing the best interests of the state as a whole, Johnson made no very radical proposals. Selectivity and mildness characterized the tax reform suggestions, caution the sections on debt and internal improvements, gradualism the proposal to end the state bank. Those who feared that the veriest leveler now occupied the governor's chair braced themselves for a litany of "cursed andyjohnsonisms" that never came. Not that Johnson had given up his national projects of homesteads and constitutional amendments—for these he briefly and politely asked legislative support—but he had resolved to devote attention to feasible solutions to immediate local problems.

Success, however, proved to be elusive. The Whigs controlled the lower house by a dozen votes; Democratic hegemony in the Senate hinged on a single vote, and there was no Immortal Thirteen to force measures through. Party discipline did not exist, and no machine stood ready at the governor's command. In the circumstances Johnson could not assemble an administration party. The legislature went its own way, ignoring most of his recommendations. Only in education did the governor's views bear significant results. Tennessee was almost last among the states in literacy, and Johnson's prodding resulted in the first law to commit state tax revenues to education, passed in February 1854.

That one notable achievement stood out on a barren landscape of neglected proposals and mandated administrative detail. Never one to shirk responsibility, Johnson took the routine seriously. He certainly could have found time to make the four-day trip home to Greeneville more often—most of his predecessors had been part-timers as a matter of course— but he frequently lamented the quantity of paperwork and suggested that his family should not look for him until they saw him coming. He made his few nominations (like the directors of the state bank), proclaimed November 24 Thanksgiving Day, named friend Milligan as Inspector General on a largely ceremonial military staff, signed numerous land grants, and corresponded with the gubernatorial neighbors on matters of extradition.

One of his few truly executive powers, the granting of pardons, brought him frequent pleas for clemency. Every convicted felon, it seemed, had youth, self-defense, excusable provocation, illiteracy, the good will of the townspeople, or an aged and widowed mother as the salient justification for mercy. Johnson pardoned more convicts than his predecessors and incurred criticism for doing so. Sometimes, however, he refused. Ninety signatures from two counties on a petition on behalf of John McBride, convicted of assault with intent to commit rape, did not impress him, particularly upon reading this explanatory endorsement by the twenty-one-year-old laborer's acquitted cohort: "Jno McBride and myself mistook the house, being drunk. it was my intention to visit a certain lewed house that I had passed the day before and asked McBride to go with me. I dont think any rudeness was offered after finding out the mistake, though to confess the truth we were both too drunk to behave right." The fellow had to stay in jail until 1859 when he had better luck with Johnson's successor.

Trivial matters and frivolous requests filled his days, and it was small wonder that in February 1855, as the next campaign neared, he sighed to David Patterson, "The thought though of canvessing the State is almost parallysing to me and especially in the heat and dust of Summer—" But he ran again. He and his party needed each other. To stand down after one depressing two-year term would have availed Johnson nothing in his quest for a national senatorship or other office. For the Democrats, distasteful though his plebeian blather was to some of the prominent, he seemed to be the most probable winner, and in Tennessee one took back-to-back victories however they offered themselves. The state convention in March unanimously nominated him "with pride and confidence," though without an endorsement of his first term.

The 1855 campaign proved to be even more taxing, physically and psychologically, than the previous one. The Know-Nothing, or Native American, movement prompted a new high of bitterness and rancor. Anti-foreign and anti-Catholic, the movement made headway as the Whig party deteriorated in the fifties, and within the South it found greatest favor in the border states. In Tennessee a coalition of Whigs and Know-Nothings supported Meredith Gentry, a state and national legislative colleague of Johnson. A ninety-day campaign involved sixty joint appearances.

Most of the standard national and state issues received at least cursory attention, but the Know-Nothing movement overshadowed all others. Johnson spared no effort in his attack on the movement. Its fear of foreigners and Catholics he called hypocritical and irrational. Tennessee's foreign population amounted to only 1 percent, and the entire state contained only three Catholic churches. Besides, he noted, all religion except the Mormon faith had foreign origins; could the Know-Nothings be expected to stop after destroying Catholicism? He defended a generous immigration policy, and talked about huddled masses of poor reaching the shores of freedom as if the Statue of Liberty already stood in New York Harbor. Nor was any of this insincere, for it extended tolerant views he had earlier expressed in Congress.

Johnson made capital of the Know-Nothings' secrecy and political oaths. Not that he opposed all forms of secrecy, for he had earlier joined the Masonic order; but he characterized the Know-Nothings as plotters who hurried with dark laterns through back alleys to political meetings at midnight, "the time at which bats retire to their hiding places, and hyenas go forth in quest of dead bodies, upon which to prey." At Manchester, just after the campaign began, he said, "Show me the dimensions of a Know-Nothing, and I will show you a huge reptile, upon whose neck the foot of every honest man ought to be placed."

Such sentiments aroused the fighting blood of Tennesseeans of all persuasions. Crowds, already heavily armed, became increasingly ugly. On one occasion rumor threatened assassination if Johnson attacked the Know-Nothings in a speech the next day. Johnson knew just what to do. Taking the platform, he observed that he preferred an orderly conduct of business at public meetings, that someone had expressed a desire to kill him, and if anyone had come for the purpose, now was the time to proceed. With that he placed his hand on his own revolver, opened his coat, and silently eyed the crowd. After a few moments of awesome stillness he said, "Gentlemen, it appears that I have been misinformed. I will now proceed to address you on the subject that has called us together." The address was not particularly mild.

A slightly smaller majority than 1853 in a slightly larger total vote put Johnson back in the statehouse for two more years. His legislative message repeated verbatim most of the 1853 document; the legislature's yawn lasted all session. They discussed homesteads only briefly and condemned Johnson's constitutional amendments as "unwise, inexpedient, and dangerous to our liberty and the perpetuity of this Union." Johnson's second term proved even more frustrating than his first. He complained to a friend, Judge William Pepper, in June 1856 about the blunders of the most "extraordinary" legislature Tennessee ever had. His Know-Nothing secretary of state also proved to be a do-nothing who sometimes went off for two weeks at a time, leaving Johnson to mind the paperwork, some of which hardly seemed gubernatorial. An 1854 law made it the governor's duty to arrange for the transportation out of Tennessee of former slaves wishing to return to Africa.

As a consequence, between February and November 1856 Johnson wrote to the American Colonization Society to confirm the frequent changes in plans to get "Hector," his wife, and two children to an acceptable seacoast destination for embarkation.

Some small episodes Johnson enjoyed. In January 1854 Judge William W. Pepper, a blacksmith before becoming circuit judge, sent him a homemade fire shovel to show his appreciation for the governor's support for mechanics. Six months later Johnson, who had long since given up tailoring as a business, responded with a handmade black coat and a letter praising artisans as the bulwark of republicanism. The correspondence, including Pepper's reply that he never had such a good fit, promptly appeared in the Nashville press.

Not only was Johnson's official position somewhat less than enthralling, but his personal life also offered sadness. When in the capital he reluctantly took rooms at the Nashville Inn rather than move his family. To son Robert he wrote, for the benefit of both Robert and Charles: "You and him have talents enough, nature has done her part if you will but do yours—" There followed a lesson on the virtues of prompt and efficient action, justice, prudence, temperance, self-reliance, and fortitude, and then an apology: "It was not my intention Sunday morning as it is, when I sit down to write a homily on morals or any other Subject. . . ." Intention or no, Johnson worried about both his grown sons, for neither of them seemed able to settle down into a profession; both had difficulties with alcohol, the oft-remarked "curse of the young men of the South," and Robert experienced continuing lung and bronchial problems.

Perhaps Johnson's concern for the older boys increased his solicitude for toddler Frank, as expressed in a letter to Martha: "He must be broke of his Conducct at the table and now is the time to do it and bashfulness with Strangers also should be correcte[d] as soon as it could be done by proper means—If he Should live and have no misfortune I think he has the elements of a very considerable man. . . . Tell mother She must not neglect that pet of ours, for we must raise him if we can—" Eliza Johnson was hardly the mother to neglect a child, but her gradually failing health—perhaps a form of slow consumption—required her to turn more and more household duties over to Martha, who in 1855 married David Patterson, a local farmer, circuit judge, and close political friend of her father. Johnson's governorship also marked the change of generations: the death of his mother and step-father and the birth of the first grandchildren.

Johnson looked forward to his infrequent trips home. He now owned the family's best residence, acquired late in his congressional service. A two-story brick building with two rooms on each floor, it was comfortable without being showy, and it would have fit the needs of many southern middle-class families. Several household servants lived in a twenty-by-thirty cabin at the rear of the lot. The acre of property included the lot and spring where the Johnsons had camped upon their first arrival in town a quarter of century before, and the sentimental Johnson opened the spring to the public. The governor who had been born in poverty now owned perhaps $10,000 worth of taxable property, including town lots and rural acreage, and he invested in government bonds as well as in railroad stock.

Near tragedy struck twice during Johnson's governorship. The Nashville Inn burned down in 1856, causing him to lose not only his belongings and $2,000 cash but also endangering his life as he rescued a helpless woman. In 1857, while he was returning from an official trip to Washington, his train derailed and rolled over a cliff, leaving Johnson with a badly mangled right arm which never healed correctly and curtailed the quality and quantity of his writing. From these and other cares Johnson sought relief in Greeneville, and there was much in the little mountain town to turn his head from politics.

Yet Johnson could never be content. Puttering in his Greeneville garden during 1856, a presidential year, he could hardly ignore the forthcoming contest. Almost certainly Johnson hoped that the state convention would make him a favorite son. That it did not reflected the bitter factional rivalries that characterized Tennessee politics. Some wanted the renomination of Pierce; others favored James Buchanan after failing to carry Aaron Venable Brown as a favorite son. The delegation went uninstructed to Cincinnati, and Buchanan got the nomination.

Although Johnson did not much care for Buchanan—called him "the Slowest man of the four" convention front runners, meaning Pierce, Lewis Cass, and even the excoriated Douglas —he campaigned for him across the state. Party loyalty provided some motivation, yet in Johnson this sentiment often clashed with a maverick tendency. The challenge of winning in a state whose national posture had for years been Whig also urged him on. Moreover, a Democratic victory in the presidential race would help return a Democratic state legislature and make possible his own election to the Senate in 1857.

At Nashville on July 15 Johnson addressed a large Democratic gathering with the most significant political speech of his governorship. He devoted a large portion of his three-hour performance to slavery. Indeed, during 1856–57 his support of slavery was as strong as it ever became. He called slavery a natural element of society throughout history, brought about because the stronger would always control the weaker and because the Negro was inferior. He defended four of the five compromise measures of 1850 and his votes for them not as compromises but as affirmations of two great principles: federal noninterference with slavery in the territories, and the people's ability to govern themselves and determine their local institutions. Thus he also supported the Kansas-Nebraska Act, because the principle of popular sovereignty opened to popular determination territory closed to slavery in 1820, thereby affirming the political power and competency of the citizen. A state constitution thus became "a mere aggregation of a portion of the power voluntarily given up by each for the good of the whole, and nothing more." One could hardly have a more individualistic view of government, and for the moment it matched the South's position on slavery in the territories, though by 1860 southern demands would be greater.

In his Nashville speech Johnson encouraged the South not to compromise away its rights but to stand united "around the altar of our common country, joined in one fraternal embrace swearing by our altars and our God that all shall sink in the dust together or this Union shall be preserved: Believing as I do, that our Southern institutions depend upon the continuance of the Union, and that the Union depends upon noninterference with our Southern institutions." That was a stronger and clearer assertion of the interdependence between slavery and the Union than Johnson had previously made, and an assertion of the necessity of Union that many of his more extreme fellow southerners denied.

Johnson's three-hour oration in Nashville, along with other efforts for Buchanan, paid off. The Democrats carried the state by 7,500 votes. Writing to Sam Milligan, Johnson observed that Buchanan's victory over Republican John C. Fremont was not "a triumph of a man, but of principle over faction and Sectionalism—" Still Johnson feared that continued efforts to elect an abolitionist president would imperil the Union.

After the presidential election Johnson's term as governor had eleven months to run. By December 1856 he told friends privately that he would not seek a third term. He thought it wise "not to pause in any place until the people become tired and restless; it is better to get out of their way a little too soon than to be in their way a little too long." Now was the time to move if he wanted the Senate. In April the Democratic state convention met, complimented Johnson for his fours years of service, and chose Isham G. Harris as the nominee for governor. Since Johnson's policies as well as national issues figured prominently in the campaign, he had hoped to speak frequently, but the painful aftermath of his January train accident forced him to curtail his activities. Nonetheless, in August the Democrats swept the prizes: governorship, seven of the ten congressional seats, and both houses of the General Assembly. A Democratic majority of twenty on joint ballot rendered certain his election as a senator, which occurred on October 8. Johnson's senatorial term had legally started on March 4, but since Congress traditionally began its work in December, his late election by the constantly off-cycle Tennessee legislature cause no practical inconvenience.

As governor, Johnson had performed the uncomplicated responsibilities of a weak office with fidelity, limited success, and high frustration. Institutional limitations, personal style, and factional rivalries permitted him to do little but mark time in the public view and then return to the national scene. The office had been "executive," but the official legacy disclosed little by way of executive handiwork. Johnson would have another opportunity within ten years—another office, with more authority, and greater problems, with more possibilities for dangerous misstep. The presidency required a high degree of preparation, and Johnson's governorship fell short of the mark. He controlled the popular vote, but the middle Tennessee aristocrats still controlled the party reins, and so each barely tolerated the other. It was hardly a propitious working arrangement, yet through it all, Johnson never lost an election. As President he would seek to marshal popular support against party leaders, and the result was even less propitious than it had been in Tennessee. A few ghosts would find their way from statehouse to White House.

V

Night and the
Tempest Close Around
1857–1862

DECEMBER 1857 had for the country many of the same characteristics that a foggy winter night has for strollers on a sea cliff. The precipice is near, and one hears the breakers below, distance and precise direction uncertain. To grope without misstep is to survive. So it was in the fog of American sectional politics, where those willing to grope toward compromise contested for leadership with those, North and South, more inclined to rush headlong come what might. Men of both styles convened in the Thirty-fifth Congress on December 4. An ominous time it was for anyone to begin a six-year term in the Senate, for by its expiration thousands of men—some under duress—would be in uniform; a presently unemployed ex-captain of infantry would be finding a way, after a year's quest, to invest Vicksburg; and those teenaged veterans who had survived the bloody heights at Fredericksburg would soon be trudging on their way to the bloody wilderness near Chancellorsville.

From his knowledge of others in the chamber (about one-third had been with him in the House) Johnson derived both encouragement and despair. His own partner, John Bell (Whig), took a moderate view of national problems, as did Kentucky's John Crittenden and the arch-patriot of Texas, Sam Houston. However, John Slidell of Louisiana, James Mason of Virginia, and the two Georgians, Robert Toombs and Alfred Iverson, had their equals in divisiveness in northerners Zachariah Chandler and Benjamin Wade. Personal vituperation would likely strain senatorial decorum, too: Jeff Davis was back. Nor did Johnson expect to see much presidential leadership, for he thought timid "Old Buck" had an insufficient "hold upon the popular heart."

The Tennesseean soon rekindled an old project: the Homestead Bill. This measure was now going on twelve years old, and whereas it had at first drawn largely scoffs, it now drew open hostility. Since 1846 the territorial question had become an increasingly divisive sectional issue. Northern pressure to keep slavery out of the territories manifested itself in the Republican party, organized for that very purpose, and southern insistence on property rights became ever more intractable. The Supreme Court's Dred Scott decision in the spring of 1857 upheld the right of planters to migrate with their slaves, untrammeled by the restrictions of congressionally enacted geographical lines. Yet if, in fact, under the encouragement of homestead legislation the territories filled up with free farmers and mechanics, there would be little room for planters, and legal protections would be of no practical value.

The cross-purposes of slavery and homesteads reached their dramatic climax in the spring of 1860, at the very point when slavery and the territorial question threatened to destroy the Democratic party. In the spring of 1858 Johnson recognized the importance of homesteads in the slavery issue. He asserted, startlingly, that a homestead policy would "reconcile" the North to slavery because homesteads meant expanding population, which in turn meant increased northern demand for cotton, rice, sugar, and tobacco. He postulated this nationalizing commonality of interest on the premise that slavery represented capital invested in labor, an economic principle both North and South could understand. The wish was father to the thought. Such reasoning availed Johnson nothing in southern delegations, where he needed votes, and a week after his speech the project got postponed till the next session.

Other topics of Johnson's first year in the Senate gave him the opportunity to expound his constitutional views. In February 1858 an administration request to increase the regular army in order to cope with a Mormon insurrection in Utah prompted him to remark that the federal government could also use troops to coerce a southern state. While debating the admission of Minnesota, Johnson warned that conceding the federal government the power to determine voting qualifications within a state meant the end of state sovereignty. That, of course, was a standard states' rights position prior to the war, and the same issue would arise in Johnson's presidency.

In the spring of 1858 the Kansas question gave Johnson an opportunity to support popular sovereignty as the best alternative to congressional determination of slavery in the territories. Since the federal government was the agent of the states, he said, it could exercise only delegated, limited powers, and it had no control over the territories for purposes other than the disposal of public land. Popular sovereignty harmonized with Johnson's belief in the people as the highest source of authority, and he supported it even when, as in Kansas, it worked badly.

As for compromise, Johnson complained that too often it infringed upon the right. He had indeed voted for four of the five compromise measures of 1850, but he always insisted he supported them because they were right in themselves. "We have been compromised and conservatised until there is hardly any Constitution left. We first compromise and settle a question wrong, and then we must all turn conservatives and stand by the wrong that has been accomplished by the compromise. Compromise! I almost wish the term was stricken out of the English language." By the winter of 1860 he would be saying the Constitution itself was the best and only "compromise" needed.

The transcontinental railroad bill in January 1859 elicited some sharp views. After pronouncing it "glaringly unconstitutional," he had fun with all the arguments in favor of it, such as the point that the flavor of Chinese tea was somehow not quite so brisk if the shipments had to dawdle through tropic climes. As for the road's strengthening the Union, " . . . this thing of saving the Union, I will remark here, has been done so often that it has got to be entirely a business proposition." Too many people "are exceedingly anxious for immortality, either in this or the other world; perhaps in both; and they must get up a great crisis; the different portions of the Union must be arrayed against each other; and it becomes necessary to save the Union. Hence there are compromises on one side and the other; and they all come up and seem to make a sacrifice on the alter of their common country, and the Union is once more saved." He had never considered the Union to be in danger, he said, and since it was in the states' interests to keep it together, he expected it to continue.

Even amidst deepening concern over the Union's future, Johnson faithfully attended to the inquiries of the "little people," who wanted their pensions, appointments, or just news of Washington. Family matters pressed. Charles, of whom his father once lamented, "God knows I have done all that I could to induce him to make a man of him self and have failed so far," tried to control his love for liquor. Johnson owned a few thousand dollars in twenty-five and thirty-year railroad bonds and continued to dabble in Greeneville real estate, but shrewdly; "There is no use in buying property unless there is a bargain [in] it," he cautioned Robert. His health still bothered him, and the arm injury sustained in the 1857 railroad accident still sent him from one doctor to another.

The social scene remained as quiet as ever. For all of Johnson's personal reserve, people sought him for speaking engagements, honorary memberships, and commissioned portraits. The Boston *Transcript*'s art critic pronounced one portrait by a local publisher "a spirited and accurate representation of a noble looking man, whose frank and open countenance bespeaks an honesty of purpose somewhat rare amongst the politicians of the present day." Upon seeing the proofs, Johnson demurred. A good "picture," yes, a good "likeness," no. The face was too smooth and youthful, and the general carriage of the body too awkward. He left the matter in the printer's hands.

While Johnson thus haggled over how he should appear on penny protrait cards, one of the grimmest visages of the age pored over maps of Virginia. John Brown, perhaps medically insane, very probably irrational, and certainly driven by religious passion, laid plans for his raid on Harper's Ferry to herald a great servile insurrection. Instead of the intended October Armageddon there occurred merely a shoot-'em-up by outraged townsfolk, followed by a little siege presided over by a federal colonel of cavalry named Robert E. Lee, assisted by a federal lieutenant of cavalry named "Jeb" Stuart and a company of Marines. In short order the Marines charged, Virginia prosecuted, and the old man stood attainted of treason, murder, and conspiracy. The hanging took place on December 2, 1859, and ten days later Senator Mason proposed a full-scale congressional investigation, though no law gave promise of restraining such as John Brown.

When Johnson took the floor, he began by criticizing Illinois Republican Lyman Trumbull. What hypocrisy, said he, to claim that the Declaration of Independence covered blacks when Illinois and many other northern states curtailed their privileges. This, of course, was a stock southern point, as was Johnson's assertion that the Constitution's three-fifths clause, rather than benefiting the South, actually penalized it for retaining slavery. As for Brown, thief, murderer, and abolitionist hero, "Those may make him a god who will, and worship him who can; he is not my god, and I shall not worship at his shrine." Neither the event nor the reaction surprised Johnson, who believed they followed logically from years of irresponsible northern pronouncements like John Quincy Adams's speeches on the "gag rule" and Seward's "irrepressible conflict" heresy. High time, said he, to stop attacking southern institutions, though he never threatened secession and in fact counseled against it.

This speech did not really measure Johnson's sectional loyalties. Brown's philosophy, and certainly his tactics, alienated everyone who, like Johnson, hoped for peaceful settlement of sectional issues. Harper's Ferry gave southern extremists another subject for speeches, but it could not by itself derange the constitutional machinery that kept the Union operating. Edmund Ruffin, the Virginia hothead, often said that in order to break up the Union, one had to break up the Democratic party. Johnson believed he was right and looked forward to the presidential year of 1860 with misgivings.

But—misgivings leavened with anticipation of opportunities. For Johnson had ambition, and he might have been a plausible compromise choice in a convention deadlocked between Douglas and one of Dixie's ultras. A border South moderate of strong Union views, Johnson faced the difficult tasks of undercutting Douglas among northern and western Democrats with the homestead and his generally populist philosophy, and convincing the far South that his constitutionalism was enough of a commitment to slavery.

Early expressions by Johnson discounted both likelihood and desire. In August 1859, in a lengthy response to an inquiry from Chattanooga's editor-postmaster, he said he "never was and never expect[ed] to be an aspirant" for the presidency. He mused, "If the presidency Could be conferred upon one who is not an aspirant as an incident flowing from the pursuit of correct principle and the Support of Sound measures Calculated in their bearing to promote our democratic form of Government and to advance the happiness, peace and prosperity of the whole people; it would then be desirable and acceptable, and in no other way—" Nomination at Charleston, let alone election, he thought impossible on such principles. He even doubted any Democratic victory unless northern attitudes on slavery changed, and since he believed that some southerners (unnamed) could get northern support, he hoped the South would unite and not acquiesce in a northern candidate.

Time and the urgings of Tennesseeans modified some of Johnson's views. His own confidants as well as middle-class friends and strangers urged him to run. Johnson's endorsement in January 1860 by the statewide Democratic convention picked up the tempo, though a few soreheads displayed countenances like "a boy who had been eating green parcimons." Now began in earnest the jockeying preparatory to Charleston. On February 8 Milligan reported high speculation about the proper course and hoped to find some "strong man" willing to block Douglas early so that Johnson could then be a compromise candidate.

In mid-March the spirit world, fascinating to Americans of this period, seemed to take particular cognizance of matters, as the San Francisco postmaster reported a transcontinental "sort of presentiment" of the senator's nomination, and a resident of Graysville, Kentucky, averred that at a seance held by a young lady of anti-Johnson persuasion John Brown's spirit had foretold his nomination. Johnson got a laugh from such tidings but seldom rewarded the authors with a reply. Indeed, he did not even write his Tennessee lieutenants as often as they wished.

Johnson kept a low profile. Even though ambitious, he disliked an unseemly rush for office. Douglas's obvious desire he found objectionable, and he had predicted in the fall of 1858 that Douglas and Seward would both try to force themselves on their respective parties. In March 1860 he described Jefferson Davis, his old austere Mississippi antagonist, as "burning up with ambition" and "nearer Consumed by an internal heat than any man I ever saw except John Slidell of La—What Jeff will do if he is not nominated God only knows—"

Davis had been doing a lot recently to focus attention directly upon slavery, in Johnson's view quite unnecessarily. On February 2, in part to undercut Douglas and improve his own position, Davis introduced a series of resolutions demanding positive federal protection for slavery in the territories and condemning all interference with it anywhere as a constitutional violation. There ensued a protracted and often rancorous debate, sometimes directly between Davis and Douglas, which, as Johnson lamented to a friend in March, would only divide the party. As passed late in May, the resolutions denied the power of either Congress or territorial legislatures to exclude slavery, thus rebuking Douglas, by that time a presidential nominee.

The Davis resolutions also complicated the course of the Homestead Bill, now at a crucial stage. The Republicans, a sectional party organized around restriction of slavery expansion, saw homesteads as a strong antislavery weapon and thus supported Johnson. But Republican votes raised the hackles of southerners and left erstwhile northern and western Democratic supporters wondering whether they ought now to become partisans and oppose what Republicans favored. Johnson needled the Republicans for satisfying the dearth of their own projects by taking up a popular Democratic one, but he accepted their backing. Since the principle was right in itself, he did not care who supported it, but he did express his "mortification" when, in April, James R. Doolittle of Wisconsin told Mason that homesteads would free the South from the immoral slave system. Of course the Virginian then had to defend slavery, and Johnson sighed, "We have been driven round and round upon the slavery question; round and round the giddy circle of slavery agitation we have gone, until our heads are reeling and our stomachs are sick, and almost heaving." Since Johnson believed that slavery would not be economically successful in much of the western territory, he often claimed that growing southern intransigence on the territories during 1858–60 thus largely protected an abstract constitutional right. This view deepened his irritation over the intrusion of slavery into the homestead question.

The homestead issue required such close watching that Johnson had to forego any inclination to visit Charleston at convention time, as he explained to Robert on April 8. He still doubted his chances: "There will be eve[r]y possible appliance brought to bear upon the convention foul and fair that is believed will have any influence whatever—" Johnson never had liked or trusted conventions because of their susceptibility to manipulation. Still, he allowed Robert to attend but cautioned him to be careful to do only what "delacacy and propriety" suggested and remember that Douglas would likely hold the upper hand, "hence the importance of occupying an acceptable position to him and his friends—"

By April 22 Robert was at Charleston, and Johnson wrote a private letter full of long-range tactics quite at variance with his earlier adamant disinterest. If "Tennessee" could get first place, hold firm, but if not—"As the matter is now before my mind I do not see how Douglas' nomination is to be Successfully resisted without great injury to the party and perhaps its overthrow"—then the vice-presidency would be worth pursuing. "If Tennessee Could Succeed now with the Second place, it would place her in the field four years hence with much assurance of Success and at the Same time be passing one of her Citizens through all the gradations of office from the lowest to highest which would be a very remarkable fact to record in history—" Caution was the watchword: "I hope you will be prudent and Say no foolish thi[n]gs which Can be used against you or me;" by all means, "mix freely" with the northwestern delegates and sound them out about "Tennessee."

Brother Charles had come too, but he mixed freely, too freely, with Charleston taverngoers, which hardly made Robert's politicking any easier. Nor were the Tennessee delegates solid. As April turned into May, a week-long string of telegrams asked Johnson's advice in various contingencies. On May 2 it appeared that Douglas had a majority (though not the required two-thirds); Johnson, asked whether Tennessee should support Douglas, replied the next day, "The delegation present, with all the facts before them are better prepared to determine what Course to pursue than I am." After the thirty-sixth ballot Johnson's name was withdrawn, and Tennessee supported Kentuckian James Guthrie. Meanwhile, across the mountains in Greeneville, the home folks had only sketchy news, and William Lowry worried, "I fear it is to end in a general muss[.]"

That it did. Charleston produced no candidate. Douglasites and Dixie firebrands demanded their own way, and when the platform fight went badly, the lower South withdrew. When the dust settled six weeks later on a series of rump conventions at Baltimore and Richmond, the erstwhile "regular" Democrats ran Douglas, while the southern Democrats chose John C. Breckinridge, currently Vice-President, and Senator Joseph Lane, a North Carolinian–become–Oregonian. Nor did Tennessee win Douglas' vice-presidential slot, either. During the interim after the Charleston debacle Johnson's allies wanted to reintroduce his name as a compromise candidate at Baltimore, but he refused "to add to the difficulties and embarrassment" of his friends and stressed the need to preserve "the only national organization remaining."

Post-mortems abounded, though less caginess and more hustle prior to Charleston would not have availed much. Perhaps loyal old Sam Milligan had it right, that the crucial point was late at Charleston when Douglas clearly could not reach two-thirds. Except for what Milligan called a "captious state of things" in the Tennessee delegation, which led to the withdrawal of Johnson's name twenty ballots before the end to avoid his being "frittered away" by delegates breaking one by one, perhaps a movement to the Tennesseean might have developed. But desire, rather than reality, often writes the script for the voice of loyalty.

Whereas the convention process crushed soft-spoken hints, the legislative process crushed strongly articulated pleas. While the Democratic party died in Charleston, the homestead died in Washington, not, however, without achieving one more milestone. The Senate passed Johnson's bill, 44 to 8, on May 10. By mid-June both houses agreed on a bill and forwarded it to President Buchanan—who vetoed it. Johnson could hardly believe what had happened. He thought that Buchanan favored the bill, and in answering the veto message, he quoted from Buchanan's inaugural address a statement supporting public land for actual settlers at moderate prices. The bill did just that, Johnson said; his earliest proposals to allow entry without cost could not overcome charges of a "giveaway." A man needed "an abiding place for his wife and for his children. Whether considerations so national, so humane, so Christian, have ever penetrated the brain of one whose bosom has never yet swelled with emotions for wife or children, is for an enlightened public to determine." An ungenerous reference to Buchanan's bachelorhood, this outburst expressed the deep frustration of a dedicated family man. The veto contained constitutional arguments that Johnson shoved aside: "When it comes to granting land by the wholesale [e.g., to railroads] and appropriating millions of acres for other purposes, the Constitution is so broad that you can drive a six-horse team and wagon clear through it anywhere."

When the Senate upheld the veto, Johnson smelled a conspiracy. Voting aye the first time were a number of southerners, including even Davis and Slidell along with the Alabamans and South Carolinians. The amendment process, which had gradually chipped away at the bill's radical "agrarianism" and left it looking like simply a bill to sell public land, may have earned some southern votes. But Davis and a number of colleagues then upheld the veto, reducing the vote to 28 to 18, and Johnson believed they had secretly connived with Buchanan on the whole affair. If Johnson supported Davis's mischievous resolutions on slavery earlier in the year to avoid losing votes on the homestead, that point, coupled with his bringing Tennessee into line for "Old Buck" in 1856, only heightened his feelings of betrayal.

Congress adjourned for the summer, and Johnson went home, more than ever in need of the revitalizing contact with friends and constituents. And they needed him. Again and again as the large crises of 1860–61 blazed into larger ones, they wrote to him, suggesting this, urging that, worrying about the future, and imploring him to keep a steady course in support of the Union. He welcomed the trust with which the most unlettered farmer addressed him on national issues. Nor were they only Tennesseeans. From the wintry plains of Hill

County, Texas, came the request, "while I am out here herding my sheep," for some documents "as will keep me up with the threatening Storm—" Other correspondents had less national interests. The ladies of Washington, Texas, wanted a contribution for their girls' school; "Clara," of "Birds Nest Cottage, Nashville," hoped for a subscription to her forthcoming volume of poetry; a 37-year-old Washington widow with a 17-year-old son hoped that Johnson, "a good and great man —ready to sympathize with women in trouble," would rent a suite of rooms from her; an isolated farmer would treasure a patent office report for evening reading; farmers' wives wanted flower seeds and tea plants from the Agriculture Department. People carried on as if nothing were awry.

But things were indeed awry, and Johnson fretted over how to set them right. The forthcoming presidential election seemed more likely to exacerbate than to heal. Everyone sought him for speeches. From West Tennessee: "In the name of our god and Country come . . . Come at all hazzards and roll back the tide. You can strike terror to the enemies of the Constitution and secure Tennsse [for] Breckenridge & Lane." But Johnson, describing his health as "irregular" and "precarious," waited until late September to enter the campaign, when he did stump for Breckinridge, having convinced himself that the Kentuckian was a Unionist. Instead, Lincoln, whom Johnson had periodically called a "Black Republican," won the national race.

Back in Washington by early December for the short lame-duck session of the Thirty-sixth Congress, Johnson found the capital alive with secessionist rumors and gloomy speculation. Since many believed secession only a matter of weeks, federal "coercion" as a response dominated every conversation. "The determination of the ultra men at this time is to involve the middle states at once upon the question of Coersion and thereby Carry them along," he informed Robert.

Constitutional amendment, solemn and seemingly permanent but slow and requiring extensive consent, appealed to many, and on December 13 Johnson proposed the same ideas

on direct election of president and senators he had supported
since 1851. An added proviso reflected current worries: every
four years, president and vice-president should alternate between slave and free states beginning with a mandated southern president in 1864. He also offered a series of amendments
on slavery, to be "unamendable," as ones on this subject now
always were, which included a geographical division of the
territories and protection of slavery in some; strengthening
the states' duty to return fugitive slaves; and prohibiting congressional interference with slavery in the District of Columbia, the interstate slave trade, or the workings of the
three-fifths clause.

Events and emotions left the Constitution, let alone potential amendments, far behind. South Carolina, unwilling to accept the results of the election, ordered a secession
convention; it met on December 17 and had a secession ordinance ready before Christmas. A winter of discontent rapidly
became a winter of decision as men reflected upon their loyalties. Some drifted helplessly, some found reasons for allowing
the tide to carry them one way or another, some stood fast and
defied the storm.

Johnson stood fast. He outraged some colleagues and surprised others, though he had often enough given clear indications that he was no disunionist, and that the South could and
should redress its grievances within the framework of the Constitution. On December 18 he erased any lingering doubts.
During discussion of his proposed amendments he denied
"the constitutionality and rightfulness of secession," as the
pamphlet version titled the speech. Yes, better Breckinridge
than Lincoln, but the election had no constitutional defects.
Yes, there had been constitutional violations by the North, but
secession, a constitutional violation itself, was hardly the
proper remedy. Yes, if oppression became unendurable, one
could invoke the "great inherent right of revolution," but
South Carolina, having put herself "in the attitude of levying
war against the United States," ought to recall that "the Con-

stitution defines and declares what is treason. Let us talk about things by their right names."

To use the right names of things often required strong language, and while Johnson was never one to shy away from that, he conceived his position to be moderate and honorable. Any southern grievances warranted cooperative southern demands for redress before precipitating revolution. He, for one, would stand by the Constitution: "I intend to cling to it as the shipwrecked mariner clings to the last plank, when the night and the tempest close around him. It is the last hope of human freedom." The last point foreshadowed Lincoln's better-known formulation of the Union as "the last, best hope of earth;" nor was it the only time he anticipated Lincoln. While agreeing that the federal government could not "coerce" a State, he asserted that it could indeed execute its laws against individuals with whatever force might be necessary, a distinction Lincoln would employ many times after Sumter.

Southerners accounted the advocacy of such a notion as the greatest heresy, but Johnson pressed on for his peroration: "Without regard to consequences, I have taken the position I have; and when the tug comes, when Greek shall meet Greek, and our rights are refused after all honorable means have been exhausted, then it is that I will perish in the last breach; yes, in the language of the [Irish rebel] patriot Emmet, 'I will dispute every inch of ground; I will burn every blade of grass; and the last intrenchment of freedom shall be my grave.' Then, let us stand by the Constitution; and in preserving the Constitution we shall save the Union; and in saving the Union, we save this, the greatest Government on earth."

Johnson's speech occupied parts of two days, and no sooner had it ended than people clamored to read it. Thousands of reprints went out; Seward wanted 5,000 to distribute; Charles Sumner, by asking for 500 copies of a speech not his own, paid it a rare compliment. Salmon Chase wrote, "Andrew Johnson is Andrew Jackson differently spelled; and I am glad to see the identity is not in name only." A few hate letters came from

Dixie; one anonymous Mississippian from Grand Junction said he had a good mind to send one of his impudent mulatto slaves to give Johnson a proper cowhiding. Johnson endorsed the envelope "Threatened assault from Mississippi. Attended to." In far-off Arkansas an editor mocked the "scurrilous old puppy, who would not fight a yearling toad frog, if he could see a chance to run," and hoped Johnson would "be made to eat Yankee nutmeg graters, until his life was grated out; and then he should be taken to a 'soap-factory' and rendered up into soap-greese, with which to wash the feet of Horace Greeley."

Tennesseeans who opposed Johnson often did not even spend the cost of a stamp. Instead they hanged and burned him in effigy, as at Memphis just before Christmas and later at Nashville. A young saddler sent Johnson a hunk of the rope used on the latter occasion along with a buckle from the vest as a "relic of that most damnable act"; other friends reminded him of John Tyler's supposed crack that burning effigies gave an honest man a good light to walk by.

Mail clerks came staggering in. Many Tennesseeans, and quite a few northerners, wrote to praise him. Clearly Unionist in sympathy, the farmers and mechanics of East Tennessee rejoiced at Johnson's stand. Although northerners thought it refreshing to have a southerner say what Johnson had said, his content followed logically from a decade of public statements; his decisiveness mirrored the crisis of the moment. A Union speech, it was also unmistakably a southern speech, with its complaints about northern aggression and insistence on southern rights. The goal, however, was still southern rights within the Union and guaranteed by the Union, because although the threat of secession was certainly greater now than Johnson had ever before admitted, he still believed a settlement possible.

Events rushed on. January brought more secessions in the Gulf South and increased tension in Tennessee. Secessionist Governor Isham Harris pressed at every turn and summoned the legislature into special session. Son Robert, a legislator since 1859, kept his father informed. The winter was bitter cold—"my ink freezes almost as fast as I can write"—and the politics bitterly hot. Some legislators hoped, unsuccessfully, to instruct Johnson on national issues, thus reviving an old tradition and an old constitutional argument. On February 9 Tennesseeans rejected a convention to consider secession, 69,000 to 58,000.

Four days earlier Johnson began another two-day effort, much of it in answer to Lane's criticism of his previous speech. He would still demand all of Tennessee's rights, "even to the ninth part of a hair," but South Carolina, presuming to speak for all, he labeled "an apple of discord in this Confederacy from my earliest recollection down to the present time, complaining of everything, satisfied with nothing." By now Charleston Harbor was a focus of national attention, and he approved Major Robert Anderson's move from Fort Moultrie to Fort Sumter as a proper defense of his men and his flag. Scorning the attacks on himself by Davis, Lane, Slidell, the mad Texan Louis Wigfall, and others, he took occasion to tamper cleverly with a bit of *King Henry VI:* "Thrice is he armed that hath his quarrel just,/ And he but naked, though locked up in steel,/ Whose conscience with secession [*Shak:* 'injustice'] is corrupted."

More than once the galleries braved the gavel of Vice-President Breckinridge to applaud the Tennesseean, especially when he said that the people could solve all the pending problems, to the discomfort of ultras at all points of the compass, if "clear propositions" were submitted to them. That notion, of course, was impossible. The formal mechanism of referendum, and then only at the state and local level, is a legacy of early twentieth-century Progressivism, and middle-period Americans knew nothing of public opinion polls. Yet the suggestion fit Johnson's long-standing philosophy of popular government, and it also revealed a particular perspective on the current crisis. He always believed that an aristocracy dominated southern politics, and he had frequently said that its leaders, for their own aggrandizement and to establish a "monarchy" if they could, would force secession against popular preference. Clearly there was no place for Johnson and his constituency in such a southern confederacy. The Union was their only hope.

Each day's mail from Tennessee confirmed Johnson's fears. Governor Harris continued to connive for secession, and postmasters made bold to interdict congressionally franked copies of pro-Union speeches. Easterners wrote about increasing fear and oppression and complained about an ineffectual national government. "Old Buck wont do for war," McDannel grumbled from Greeneville on February 16. "He is afraid somebody might get hurt."

"May God and the people Save the Country—for I fear Congress will not," Johnson had written in January, and the waning days of the session confirmed his view. Compromise measures acceptable to both sides could not be found, and the chambers became increasingly chaotic. When on March 2, two days before Lincoln's inaugural, Johnson spoke in reply to more of Joe Lane's fulminations and said, "Show me who has been engaged in these conspiracies, who has fired upon our flag, has given instructions to take our forts and our customhouses, our arsenals and our dock-yards, and I will show you a traitor," there followed throaty huzzahs in the galleries, parliamentary pandemonium on the floor over attempted remedial action by the chair, and a gallery-clearing order that took ten minutes to execute.

The crisis at Sumter came in mid-April, by which time Congress had adjourned and Johnson was preparing to leave for Tennessee. His railroad ride through Virginia tested his mettle, for at several points rebel crowds threatened the train; it passed through Bristol without stopping, supposedly on orders from President Davis, to prevent a politically counterproductive lynching. By the end of April Johnson reached Greeneville, whence he set out on a speaking tour of East Tennessee with several noted Whigs who had joined the Union cause. Violence shadowed the party; while speaking in a church at Kingsport he kept a revolver on the pulpit, politely covered with a handerchief, but nothing happened.

Meanwhile, Lincoln's call for troops induced Governor Harris to sign a military pact with the Confederacy and the legislature to appoint June 8 as the day for a popular vote on secession. Though the eastern counties favored the Union by two to one, statewide results favored secession by a margin of 55,000 votes, and Johnson called the whole thing a fraud. By late June Harris declared the state out of the Union, and Johnson's friends urged him to flee to save himself from arrest or assassination. He did, traveling in an open carriage on country roads, having left his family behind.

This most galling trip of Johnson's life ultimately brought him back to Washington, where Lincoln had summoned Congress into special session beginning July 4. Ratification of presidential emergency measures since April topped the legislative agenda. In a major speech on July 27 Johnson strongly supported Lincoln's course. He cited historical precedents for most of Lincoln's actions and pronounced them "justified by the great law of necessity." To those who complained about violations of the Constitution he replied that "a violation of the Constitution for the preservation of the Government, is more tolerable than one for its destruction." War having been forced upon the government, it was clearly the president's constitutional duty to resist the moves of "the pseudo-hermaphrodite government that has been gotten up down there." Remembering Bull Run six days earlier, he said: "Though your flag may have trailed in the dust; though a retrograde movement may have been made; though the banner of our country may have been sullied, let it still be borne onward; and if, for the prosecution of this war in behalf of the Government and the Constitution, it is necessary to cleanse and purify that banner, I say let it be baptized in fire from the sun and bathed in a nation's blood! The nation must be redeemed; it must be triumphant. The Constitution—which is based upon principles immutable, and upon which rest the rights of man and the hopes and expectations of those who love freedom throughout the civilized world—must be maintained."

"Cleanse and purify"—abolitionists talked that way. But as the Senate showed by adopting, 30 to 5, the war aims resolution Johnson introduced, this was not a war to abolish slavery. Although forced upon the country by southern "disunionists," the war would nevertheless be prosecuted not "in any spirit of oppression, nor for any purpose of conquest or subjugation, nor for the purpose of overthrowing or interfering with the rights or established institutions of those States," rather to preserve the Constitution and the Union "with all the dignity, equality, and rights of the several States unimpaired," and "as soon as these objects are accomplished the war ought to cease." Combining the dominant view of war guilt with a moderate statement of intended policy, this resolution, helpful now in keeping the border states in the Union, would return to influence Johnson's thoughts and actions at the end of the war.

For the moment, however, marshaling the nation's power took precedence over expounding its philosophy, and Johnson's attention focused on east Tennessee. "We will stand as long as we can," he said of his countrymen, "and if we are overpowered, and liberty shall be driven from the land, we intend before she departs, to take the flag of our country, with a stalwart arm, and a patriotic heart, and an honest tread, and place it upon the summit of the loftiest and most majestic mountain. We intend to plant it there, and leave it, to indicate to the inquirer who may come in after times, the spot where the Goddess of Liberty lingered and wept for the last time, before she took her flight from a people once prosperous, free, and happy."

Lying astride the main east-west rail line supplying Virginia, and one of the most prominent pockets of Union sentiment anywhere in Secessia, east Tennessee had vital strategic significance to both sides. The Confederates moved quickly to occupy it and control the population. Johnson cited his correspondents as proof of a "reign of terror" and clamored for relief in the form of money, arms shipments, and if necessary a military invasion. Union efforts faltered, however. A Union army could not get at east Tennessee except through Kentucky, tottering in precarious "neutrality" during the summer, and by the time that state became a usable base of operations, overcautious generals such as Don Carlos Buell could make no headway against Confederate defenses.

Late summer and autumn of 1861 were one long speaking tour, mostly in Ohio and Kentucky, to boost Union morale and aid recruiting. The December session of Congress brought Johnson back to the capital, where he served on the Joint Committee on the Conduct of the War, whose ardent Republican members sought to preserve a congressional function in the shaping of military policy.

Finally, affairs in Tennessee began to brighten. In January 1862 came news that the family was headquartered at son-in-law Dan Stover's farm in Carter County and mostly safe, though Charles, Robert, and Dan had been flirting with danger by helping to organize regiments of Tennessee Unionists in Kentucky and harassing Confederate occupation forces. Johnson having been declared an "alien enemy" by the legislature, his property was seized and his house made into a rebel hospital. Then, in February, Ulysses Grant acquired Forts Henry and Donelson in west Tennessee (and the nickname "Unconditional Surrender"), thus obliging Confederate General Albert Sidney Johnston not only to abandon any plans for Kentucky but to evacuate Nashville as well. These swells in the tides of war cut off Senator Johnson's term one year before its end and thrust him into a new and even more taxing post.

Johnson's service in the Senate began with his conviction that sectional conflict could be averted by adherence to the Constitution, and ended with his dedicated participation in a full-scale military enterprise to preserve a Union he always asserted could not legally be destroyed. He started out an anomalous southerner: a plebeian slaveowner who harped about democracy and homesteads, and thought the slaves he gained by honest toil a more valid form of wealth than the slaves inherited by aristocratic planters' sons; a slaveowner who talked a good talk about southern rights, but whose silence during senatorial threats to fight a good fight over them inclined the suspicious to watch him. He ended up an anomalous southerner still, or more precisely a "traitorous" southerner or a "good" southerner, depending on one's point of view. Believing himself in 1857 to be a traditional mainline Democrat and still hoping in 1860 that Breckinridge could reflect enough of those values and enough Union loyalty to win, by 1862 he found himself supporting, if not consorting with, a Republican president and being praised by the likes of Ben Wade and Charles Sumner. Insisting always that the Constitution was a fixed star by whose color, brightness, and position one could navigate, he agreed to become himself rather like an asteroid, a constitutional oddity, a presidentially appointed Military Governor of Tennessee.

In December 1857 Johnson came to the United States capitol knowing that he had got there in spite of the bilious maledictions of a Knoxville editor, that rascal Whig whose years of enmity gave him senior rank among Johnson's nemeses, "Parson" Brownlow. In March 1862 Johnson came to the newly liberated Tennessee capitol and according to popular stories shortly encountered on its steps the same Parson Brownlow, just released from the jail cell where his now fiercely pro-Union columns had induced the irritated Confederates to lodge him. So much had they suffered in the same cause that they fell into each other's arms and wept. "Well, I never!" said the passers-by, and not long before, Johnson thought he never would, either. But he firmly believed that consistency brought him to that day, consistency in upholding principles that were to him unquestionably correct. Whether he would give Brownlow credit for equal consistency remained uncertain. For the moment, however, any hand was welcome in a war to save his country.

V I

Striking Down
the Tall Poppies
1862–1865

IF, as people said, the Civil War was a brothers' war,
Andrew Johnson knew just how that was so. Back in February
1861, as Texas prepared to hold a popular election on secession, Johnson's long-absent brother William penned a rambling, sorrowful letter. After expressing an intention to vote
for secession, he said: "I expect to live and die in Brazoria
County Texas [.] my Brother I want you to receive in this letter
the wormest Love of a Brother to his brother as long as mortal
life shall last [.] answer my letter and let me here from you as
I never Expect to see you in life [.]" Not only had secession
divided his own family, but now Andrew Johnson in the uncertain spring of 1862 returned to govern by force his adopted
Tennessee, where perhaps more than in any other state families knew how cruelly divisive the war could be.

A bothersome misfit before, Johnson was now the symbol,
and the anticipated reality, of tyranny. He represented power
in all its most ominous dimensions: without precedent,
vaguely defined, clearly supported by higher authority, and
wielded by a previously frustrated executive known for single-

minded tenacity. During more peaceful times Johnson had shown a special regard for constitutional niceties which the currents of war at least in part eroded. Together with Lincoln he foreshadowed a view of the war power supported by the twentieth-century Supreme Court: that when the security of the nation was at stake, the Constitution made available the fullest measure of resources necessary to its survival. Yet Johnson still retained elements of a states' rights philosophy that would surface again during his presidency. War might derange, but not destroy, the consistency of beliefs deeply held.

Johnson arrived in Nashville with a couple of trunks and very little official baggage. His appointment gave him the authority to exercise "all and singular the powers, duties, and functions pertaining to the office of military governor"—not a very informative grant. The concept of a military governor for forcefully repossessed American territory was unheard of, and the domestic nature of the conflict blurred the traditional rights of an occupying power under international law. Rather than give specific instructions, the War Department told Johnson that it would rely on his "sound discretion to adopt such measures as circumstances may demand." Both Johnson and his Washington superiors had to feel their way through much uncharted legal and political terrain. Johnson also brought with him the rank of brigadier general, United States Volunteers, a personal as well as official anomaly. He could not perform his functions without the support of the army, and the government thought he might have better relations with the generals if he were one of them—at least on paper.

Lincoln dispatched Johnson to begin the process of restoration (a contemporary and more descriptive synonym for reconstruction) of loyal civil government. Successful restoration required popular election of loyal officials, which in turn required a secure countryside. That meant the expulsion of all Confederate military forces from the state. However, geography and the fortunes of war seldom smiled on the Union in Tennessee. The eastern portion, strongly Unionist, came early under a tight Confederate rule by which, as Johnson lamented,

"Our people are oppressed and pursued as beasts of the forest." The western part, ardently Confederate, came earliest under Union occupation following the capture of Forts Henry and Donelson in February 1862, the incredibly bloody and lucky victory at Shiloh in April, and the capture of Memphis in June. Middle Tennessee witnessed extensive operations by both armies, and not until late 1864 was Nashville itself safe from the threat of Confederate incursions.

Johnson started off with a proclamation. The United States would carry out "its high constitutional obligation to guarantee to every state in this Union a republican form of government." To Johnson, "state" meant the loyal citizens thereof, and whether few or many, they embodied the indestructible sovereignty of the state within the Union and could summon federal aid and protection. A "republican" form of government meant a loyal one chosen by the people through the elective franchise. The guaranty clause from Article IV served as the main constitutional underpinning for federal efforts to restore civil government, and Johnson frequently cited it as his administration progressed.

Johnson spoke a mixture of firmness and conciliation: "Those who through the dark and weary nights of the rebellion have retained their allegiance to the Federal government will be honored. The erring and misguided will be welcomed on their return. And while it may become necessary in vindicating the violated majesty of the law and reasserting its imperial sway to punish intelligent and conscious treason in high places, no merely retaliatory or vindictive policy will be adopted." In prose more ornate than Lincoln would have used, this statement represented the President's views: no harsh punishment and a "full and complete amnesty for all past acts and declarations" to those who would promise to be loyal in the future. It was only the most general outline of a "presidential plan" of reconstruction.

Eager to get moving, Johnson busied himself during the spring of 1862 by reopening civil courts under military protection and by appointing interim local and statewide officials.

Within his limited geographical sphere of control he purged secessionist judges, city councilmen, mayors, and state bank officials. The press and the clergy, for their obvious influence on public opinion, bore close watching. At least one editor found himself behind bars and his editorial rooms padlocked; in June the governor haled before him six clergymen accused of preaching treason from the pulpit. Since these "assumed ministers of Christ" would not recant and take the oath, he sent one to jail and several others to the North, one of them adjuring well-wishers at the station not to forget God, Jeff Davis, and the Confederacy.

Johnson noted with pleasure that Grant's nip-and-tuck victory at Shiloh in April had buoyed the loyalists and dismayed the rebels. Ten days after that bloody Sunday he enthused to Washington, "All is working well in this part of Tennessee, beyond my most sanguine expectations." Business in Nashville picked up, the price of cotton rose, and trains on the L & N came chuffing in every day.

Johnson's impatience to redeem his adopted state and Lincoln's hope for prompt results led him to hazard an election on May 22 for a local judgeship in the Nashville circuit. The outcome proved anything but "sanguine." One of the brashest secessionists won by 200 votes; Johnson, crafty in his mortification, formally installed him in office but arrested him the next day and appointed the defeated Unionist in his stead. The whole episode left the rebels laughing.

Lincoln, disappointed, kept quiet for a month and then started hinting again. On July 3 he wrote, "If we could, somehow, get a vote of the people of Tennessee and have it result properly it would be worth more to us than a battle gained. How long before we can get such a vote?" Johnson replied that upon the liberation of east Tennessee there would be "an expression of public opinion that will surprise you." In April he had predicted that as soon as the state was free of graycoats, "Tennessee will be for the Union by 70,000 votes." If Johnson's patriotism led him to exaggerate, he at least recognized the necessary order of events: successful battles before successful ballots. He could appoint officials by the platoon, but if Union regiments could not clear the state and secure the countryside from guerilla raids, the officials could not function, and Unionists would keep silent in the face of Southrons' bravado.

Johnson's awareness that the army was the key to this work only heightened his frustrations, for throughout 1862 conflicts of jurisdiction and personality fostered disharmony with officers at all levels from senior command to local provost marshals. Generals Don Carlos Buell and Henry Halleck shared responsibility for Tennessee. Both tended to plod, hardly to the liking of the impetuous governor, and Halleck in addition had Johnson's own imperious and grating personality, though with a more erudite veneer. In April Johnson complained, "Petty jealousies and contests between generals wholly incompetent to discharge the duties assigned them have contributed more to the defeat and embarrassment of the Government than all other causes combined." Lincoln, dodging a hail of telegrams, gently commented to Johnson that he could not grant all of his demands without simply putting him in supreme military command in Tennessee. To the prickly Halleck, Lincoln described Johnson as "a true and valuable man —indispensable to us in Tennessee."

The situation in the field deepened Johnson's worries and shortened his patience. When Union armies concentrated at one point, they left only sparse garrisons elsewhere, and during the spring and summer campaigns of 1862 Johnson became alarmed at what he regarded as the defenseless conditon of Nashville. He pleaded for the return of units from Halleck's army; Halleck, nearly (and finally) ready to move on the rebels at Corinth, in northern Mississippi, responded crossly to the War Department, "We are now at the enemy's throat, and cannot release our great grasp to pare his toenails." Throughout the summer Bedford Forrest and John Morgan took turns sweeping through middle Tennessee with cavalry and between mid-September and mid-November the rebels laid siege to the capital. The befuddled Buell seemed

unable to cope with the situation, and Johnson set about marshaling jittery citizens and hastily impressed slaves. Lincoln
and Secretary of War Edwin Stanton eventually saw the force
of Johnson's long-continued criticism of Buell, and on October 24 General William S. Rosecrans took over. Rosecrans
promptly advanced on Nashville with reinforcements; the
rebels backed off; and Buell repaired to Cincinnati to sweat out
a five-month court of inquiry. The court accorded Johnson the
honor of saving Nashville, censured Buell's conduct on several
counts, and sent him home, "waiting orders" that never came.

Whether or not Johnson saved Nashville single-handedly,
he had certainly been busy recruiting troops and, by delegation from Lincoln, deciding terms for the release of individual
Tennesseans charged with aiding the rebellion. Typical of
Johnson's attitude was his arrest of "seventy vile secessionists
in this vicinity" to trade for seventy "respectable and valuable"
east Tennesseans languishing in Mobile Prison. Those who
refused exchange he deported southward at their own expense; better to lay upon rebels the burden of feeding their
own than to crowd northern prisons. Indeed, Johnson's early
willingness to try leniency had hardened. "We have all come
to the conclusion here that treason must be made odious and
traitors punished and impoverished," he wrote to Lincoln on
July 26. "I am doing the best I can."

Johnson's "best" often had more than a little tinge of arbi-
trariness. According to the post commander at Murfreesboro,
Tennesseans hated Johnson personally. They could not single out any unwarranted official action, "but still, either in
manner of doing it, or that it should be done by him, or from
some undefinable course touching him, their resentment is
fierce and vindictive." This evaluation in July 1862 by an officer with whom Johnson had clashed echoed the fears of Assistant Secretary of War Thomas A. Scott at the time of Johnson's
appointment. Writing to Stanton from Nashville, Scott had
worried that Johnson's prewar course in Tennessee, his stand
in the secession crisis, and his actions since, would prevent his
many opponents from cooperating in restoration. Johnson, he

feared, would become a specific object of secessionist attack or even assassination.

Yet Lincoln always supported Johnson, even when the governor ordered that for every harassed Unionist at least five prominent local "secesh" were to be "arrested, imprisoned, and otherwise dealt with as the nature of the case may require," or when his views on the confiscation of rebel property to repay despoiled Unionists outstripped the provisions of federal law. Despite Johnson's regular demands for the removal of post commanders, provost marshals, and staff officers, Lincoln thought Johnson the best of the three current military governors and said in the summer of 1862 that the Tennesseean had never done anything to embarrass him.

One crucial reason why Lincoln needed Johnson in Tennessee was emancipation. Even though a slaveowner himself, if the choice were slavery or the Union, he told a Nashville audience on the Fourth of July, "I say, in the face of Heaven, give me my government and let the negro go!" In September Lincoln's preliminary proclamation of emancipation gave rebels an opportunity to keep their slaves by bringing their states back into the Union. They could evidence their loyalty by electing representatives to Congress, which Lincoln would take as a conclusive showing that the particular state was no longer in rebellion.

Wartime elections in Tennessee were a tenuous business at best, but on October 21 Lincoln urged Johnson and the army to support the effort: "In all available ways give the people a chance to express their wishes at these elections. Follow law, and forms of law as far as convenient; but at all events get the expression of the largest number of the people possible." To satisfy Lincoln and local Unionists as well, Johnson on December 8 ordered an election in two West Tennessee congressional districts. Nothing went right, however; a mass meeting to choose candidates also produced resolutions against emancipation and demands that Washington repay citizens for property damages caused by the Union army. Then Bedford Forrest took his Confederate cavalry tearing through the region, preventing the polls from opening at all. One embarrassment thus averted another, and Johnson threw up his hands in despair.

Lincoln's final New Years' edict of emancipation did not apply to Tennessee, omitted from the proclamation's list of states in rebellion. The omission showed the harmony of Lincoln's and Johnson's desires. The exclusion of Tennessee elevated a fiction into an official truth: that significant progress in restoration had taken place. The exclusion also accommodated Johnson's strong belief that as long as some Tennesseans remained loyal, the state remained intact within the Union, and secession had no constitutional effect. In addition, it matched Johnson's constitutional views on slavery as a state matter. As he had defended before the war a state's right to have slavery, so he now preferred emancipation in Tennessee to come at the hands of a freely chosen and forthright state legislature—and so, as president, would he wish to consign legislation on race relations to the states.

Having pretended that Tennessee was no longer tainted with rebellion, Lincoln now longed for some snappy military victories. The same newspapers that announced and editorialized about emancipation reported Rosecrans' defeat of Braxton Bragg at Murfreesboro on January 2 after four days of bloody, muddy grappling. Eagerly Lincoln wanted to know the effect. Johnson wired back that the battle had convinced Unionists they would ultimately win. "Ultimately" proved to mean another year, for during the entire spring Rosecrans sat at Murfreesboro watching Bragg, who sat at Tullahoma protecting the vital communication center of Chattanooga. Only cavalry was active, but the six-month occupation of middle Tennessee by two armies totalling over 100,000 men made progress at restoration impossible.

Johnson, increasingly irritated, toured Ohio, Pennsylvania, New York, and New Jersey in February, stumping for Union and emancipation. He asserted that after the war the black man would have to meet the same standards imposed on others, which for this champion of yeomen and mechanics meant hard work, frugality, and social responsibility: "If he can rise by his own energies, in the name of God, let him rise!"

In March 1863 Lincoln noted rumors that the governor was thinking about recruiting blacks to serve in the Union army, and he hoped that "some man" of Johnson's "ability, and position" would take up the task. "If you *have* been thinking of it please do not dismiss the thought." Johnson recruited blacks primarily as laborers on fortifications, whereas the army wanted them all in training camps. In September the War Department directed recruiters not to act contrary to the governor's wishes.

Black troops were not the only source of civil-military friction during the tenure of General Rosecrans, whom Johnson personally liked. Strained relations, especially over government contracts and arrest of civilians, continued until the War Department offered a general outline of civil and military jurisdiction, and in June 1863 a friendly letter from Johnson patched up the quarrel. The governor concluded on a personal matter: "Please accept my thanks for the gentle admonition you gave my son, and the kind manner in which it was done."

It was either going to be a gentle admonition or else a general court-martial for Robert, now a colonel and still an alcoholic, who could not manage the heady chemistry of bottle and braid. Eager to be promoted a flag officer even though his cavalry regiment, sans saddles, was still training in Ohio, he racked up one instance of "conduct unbecoming" after another, which required the intercession of his second in command (curious business — Parson Brownlow's son helping Andy Johnson's son out of a scrape) and his brother-in-law Dan Stover, now also a colonel. Before long he resigned his commission and became an aide to his father. As if Robert's irresponsibility was not enough for Eliza Johnson, put out of her home by rebels and seriously ill with consumption, her favorite son Charles had died of head injuries when thrown from an unruly horse in April, and young Frank had developed tuberculosis. What sadness war did not visit upon the Johnsons, nature seemed waiting to supply.

A brief respite of sorts came in June 1863 when Johnson traveled to Washington to help plan the long-awaited invasion of east Tennessee by General Ambrose Burnside. By August the governor, back in Nashville, once again faced the prospect of elections. Statewide balloting properly occurred in August of odd years. Some Unionists urged Johnson to set the machinery in motion, but in addition to the presence of Confederate armies another problem now loomed—dissension within Unionist ranks. Emancipation had generated a conservative faction which opposed Johnson personally and accused him of greater devotion to "the cause of the negro than to the cause of peace." The conservatives demanded a statewide election, and when Johnson concluded not to risk it, they held their own in several counties. Except for highlighting a split that would soon widen, and exemplifying charges that Johnson wished to become a dictator, the election was meaningless.

Shortly, however, the situation began to brighten. By the first week in September Rosecrans had chased Bragg beyond Chattanooga and through the mountains into Georgia, while Burnside seized Knoxville. With Tennessee now clear of Confederates for the first time, Johnson promised: "Many humble men, the peasantry and yeomanry of the South, who have been decoyed, or perhaps driven into the rebellion, may look forward with reasonable hope for an amnesty. But the intelligent and influential leaders must suffer. The tall poppies must be struck down."

The tramp of armies perked Lincoln up. On September 11 he called the moment "the nick of time" for a push toward restoration. Methods he left to Johnson, just so that only trustworthy, loyal men participated and that the friends of Union rather than Isham Harris and his Confederate crew emerged victorious. Lincoln agreed with Johnson's position that the guaranty clause in Article IV of the Constitution conferred the authority to act to restore a "republican form of government" that would qualify for federal recognition and protection. Lincoln also gave Johnson the go-ahead for "making" a new state constitution if he thought it desirable and necessary to secure emancipation. Lincoln clearly intended Johnson to have a free hand and ample authority, and Johnson expected to hold elections for governor, legislature, and congressional seats in December.

Suddenly the military situation deteriorated. Bragg, reinforced, caught an unwary Rosecrans at Chickamauga, where only George Thomas's rocklike character saved the day. The rebels retrieved part of east Tennessee. Rosecrans lost his command to Thomas, one of Johnson's few favorites, and the whole western theater came under Ulysses Grant, who by Thanksgiving had forced Bragg out of Tennessee for good with decisive victories at Lookout Mountain and Missionary Ridge and then detached William T. Sherman to rescue Burnside. Perhaps at last restoration was at hand.

On December 8 a presidential amnesty proclamation offered Tennessee and other Confederate states a path to reunion. Except for high-ranking rebels and those who deserted federal civil or military positions to make war, anyone guilty of rebellion could have a full pardon and restoration of property other than slaves by taking an oath of future loyalty. When in any state a number of voters equal to 10 percent of the votes cast in 1860 had taken the oath and formed a loyal, "republican" state government, Lincoln (though not necessarily Congress) would recognize and protect it in accordance with the guaranty clause. Lincoln concluded his own proposal by adding, "It must not be understood that no other possible mode would be acceptable."

In fact, Johnson had in mind a more stringent variation. To a mass meeting at the capitol in Nashville on January 21, 1864 he outlined his expectations of rebels, each of whom was "by his own act, expatriated." Anyone who simply wanted pardon could ask for clemency at "President Lincoln's altar, " but the franchise would require "a hard oath—a tight oath." He favored immediate emancipation, bluntly suggested the desirability of dividing up large plantations into family farms, and observed, "If the negro is better fitted for the inferior condition of society the laws of nature will assign him there." The meeting supported Johnson and authorized him to call a state constitutional convention whenever the entire state could be represented.

A proclamation on January 26 revealed that the "hard oath" for voters meant swearing that one consciously desired the overthrow of secession and would work for it; a mere promise of loyalty was not enough. Lincoln believed the original oath sufficient for voting but acquiesced in Johnson's judgment, observing that the governor had not deviated from his position "to any ruinous extent." Statewide elections for local officers on March 5 nearly proved ruinous, however. Over half the counties succeeded in electing officers but amidst so many irregularities and such factional opposition and boycotting that the results proved only that Johnson had a badly divided Union party.

Undaunted, Johnson turned to his east Tennessee friends for support in the next step—the approaching Republican national convention. A series of irregular meetings across the state in May chose delegates, supported the national war policy, and urged Lincoln's reelection. They also endorsed Johnson for vice-president, though he apparently did not instigate this action. At Baltimore the Republicans accepted the Tennesseeans and then chose Johnson as Lincoln's running mate.

Johnson's nomination reflected perfectly the nature of Lincoln's war coalition. A Democrat, a southerner, a loyal slaveholder converted to emancipation, a consistent Unionist, Johnson was in many respects the ideal candidate. Lincoln had him in mind before the convention because he sent General Daniel Sickles, a one-legged war hero, to Nashville in May to check out Johnson's personal habits. Sickles was quite a choice for such a mission, in view of his involvement in an infamous murder triangle before the war and his amorous dalliances with the ex-Queen of Spain while a diplomat after the war, but he gave Johnson a clean report, and Lincoln manifested no further doubts.

As election day approached, irregularities became the regular order in Tennessee. A meeting of "citizens" at Nashville in August requested a state convention; Johnson obliged and called one, which met in September and comprised largely self-selected, pro-Johnson delegates. In preparation for the presidential election the convention once more escalated the requirements for voting. Now one had to have been a Union volunteer or else be a "known active friend" of the government who rejoiced in its victories, opposed a negotiated peace, and promised to "heartily aid and assist the loyal people in whatever measures may be adopted" to win the war. Even so, election officials could reject suspected rebels no matter what they swore.

Such regulations ensured that only unconditional Johnson Unionists would be able to vote; in October Lincoln abruptly rejected the protest of a delegation supporting General George McClellan, his opponent, and huffily accused them of being in league with the New York Democratic machine. Johnson made no campaign appearances outside Tennessee and few within. He did speak to a torchlight procession of blacks on the night of October 24; by all accounts he was highly demagogic and may have promised to "indeed be your Moses, and lead you through the Red Sea of war and bondage to a fairer future of liberty and peace." The election held no surprises. Increased cavalry raids in preparation for General John Hood's last Confederate invasion of the state prevented an election in many areas. Disaffected citizens refused to vote even when they could. Lincoln got an overwhelming majority of a tiny vote, but Congress, ruling that no constitutional election had occurred, discounted Tennessee's electoral votes. Lincoln said nothing.

George Thomas's crushing defeat of Hood near Nashville on December 15–16 ended the last rebel hopes for Tennessee, and restoration could then proceed unhindered. The Johnson men determined to control, no matter how irregular the process. Easterners called for a statewide constitutional convention, and on January 9, 1865 a motley array of 500 delegates met in Nashville, some having been chosen by mass meetings, others by the Tennessee regiments in which they served. For three days the assemblage wrangled over its authority: was it a legitimate convention itself, or should it propose a regularly elected one? On the night of the twelfth Johnson urged the convention to draft several "simple propositions," chief among which was abolition of slavery, and submit them for popular ratification. Here his long-standing idea of popular sovereignty proved very useful; whatever the people ultimately ratified was constitutional, never mind any untidy preliminaries. "Suppose you do violate the law," he said, "if by so doing you restore the law and the constitution, your consciences will approve your course, and all the people will say amen!" It was Johnson's greatest deviation from his usual scrupulous regard for detail.

Thus inspired, the remaining delegates (not quite 300) abolished slavery, voided secession and subsequent acts of the Confederate state legislature, approved Johnson's actions, and ordered two elections, one on February 22 to ratify the convention's work and another on March 4 to choose a governor and legislature. Modifications of the franchise, including partial extension to blacks, they left to the legislature—but of course nobody could vote in the two forthcoming elections without taking the current stringent oaths. The turnout was overwhelming in sentiment but underwhelming in numbers— though it did reach a "10 percent" showing by Lincoln's definition—and William G. Brownlow, once at Johnson's throat but more recently at his side, took the gubernatorial chair. "Thank God the tyrant's rod is broken," Johnson telegraphed to Lincoln.

The breaking had required considerable effort, which at times bore heavily on Johnson's physical and emotional strength, as it tested his political skills and his philosophy of power. A debilitating fever had wracked him for several weeks in early 1865. The war had severely deranged his family life. More important, however, was the frustrating nature of his second executive experience. His first governorship, during a period in which state power was primary and national power secondary, saw Johnson in a position in which he had a personal following but no personal, institutional power to accomplish his programs. His second governorship, during a war over the location of the boundaries between state and national power, and in which he was the agent of a President who used and told him to use all power necessary to preserve the Union, found him with a seriously embattled personal following and little opportunity to quickly accomplish his tasks. Only the preservation of the Union from the aggressions of an "arrogant aristocracy, based upon human bondage" and scornful of "honest industry and personal worth" made it more satisfying than the first.

Always there seemed a stumbling block. In his first governorship it was a balky legislature, in his second a pokey Union army. Impetuous and hard driving by nature, he resented challenge and disagreement, which seemed only to convince him of his righteousness and encourage him to persevere. During the Civil War his perseverance succeeded, and in accepting his resignation as military governor, Stanton commented on the Union for which the Tennesseean had "so long and so gallantly periled all that is dear to man on earth." Surely, Johnson thought, the vice-presidency would be an end of peril.

On February 25 Johnson started for Washington, where he arrived three days before inauguration day. On the night of March 3 Senate Secretary John W. Forney held a "jollification" in his capitol office for ex-Democrats (like himself) in the Lincoln administration. Notables came and went, including Salmon Chase, Gideon Welles, and William Seward. Johnson, who had not intended to go, found the company and conversation relaxing, partied till after midnight, and woke up on inauguration morning with a hangover and perhaps a recurrence of his recent fever. Gradually he improved, but after arriving at the capitol to take the oath, he again felt unsteady and resorted to a drink of whiskey to calm himself. His inaugural speech in the Senate chamber comprised fifteen minutes of incoherent, drifting homilies about the agonies of war and the beauties of popular government, with much ado about his own plebeian origins. After witnessing this sorry, poor-boy-made-good performance, Lincoln sighed and went out on the portico for his own "malice towards none" exhortation—and adopted that same attitude towards his new Vice-President, whom he never publicly criticized and often defended in private. Politicians and press alike heaped abuse on Johnson, however, and so he went to the estate of old-line Democratic politico Francis Preston Blair in nearby Maryland for a while. The Senate being out of session, there was nothing particularly to do in Washington.

As Carl Schurz, writing long afterward, would remember the Johnson of 1863, "To hear him expatiate upon this, his favorite theme [punishment], one would have thought that if this man ever came into power, the face of the country would soon bristle with gibbets, and foreign lands swarm with fugitives from the avenging sword of the Republic. And such sentiments he uttered not in a tone betraying the slightest excitement, but with the calmness of longstanding and unquestionable conviction." Perhaps at the Blairs', in the rural quiet of Silver Spring, Johnson reflected upon his future. For all he knew, such questions of power were Lincoln's alone until 1869. Except that a mad actor was reflecting upon how to embark the country upon a different course.

VII

Proclamations, Pardons, and Parties

1865

THE APRIL NIGHT gave every evidence of being a good one for sleeping. Sounds of victory celebrations from the streets below seemed strangely muffled by the damp mist, which developed into a chilly drizzle before morning. Andrew Johnson, having declined a friend's invitation to share main-floor seats at Ford's Theater, read for a while in the parlor of his suite at the Kirkwood House on Pennsylvania Avenue and then went to bed, the lingering effects of his illness encouraging sleep. Before eleven an insistent, heavy-handed banging on the door roused him to greet his theatergoing friend, who brought word that President Lincoln lay near death from an assassin's bullet. Johnson dressed and after some uncertainty decided to go to the house across from Ford's where officials were slowly gathering at Lincoln's bedside. Concerns for his own safety as well as other considerations dictated a short visit, and Johnson returned to his rooms to await further report. By seven-thirty Lincoln was gone. The Tennesseean had become an executive for the third time.

On paper, at least, Johnson showed remarkable qualifications. Alone among the first seventeen presidents, Johnson had served in a governorship, both houses of a state legislature, and both houses of Congress. His nearest rival was John Tyler, whose presidency proved to be one escalating crisis from beginning to end. Yet no amount of prior service could guarantee success with the complex issues of Reconstruction. Not only did the aftermath of a civil war present unique constitutional problems, but the political context in which those issues arose had no precedent in Johnson's personal history.

Reconstruction was not so much a period in American history as it was a process by which the South's temporarily deranged "proper practical relations" to the Union, in Lincoln's words, could be restored. States had to be restored to representation in Congress, day-to-day functions of the federal government had to be restored in the South, and individual rebels restored to their loyalty. None of these minimal results, let alone the more sweeping interests of some northerners in confiscation of property, expansion of suffrage, extensive social reform, and military occupation, could occur unless the federal government took action. Thus, all of the specific issues of Reconstruction merged in the unifying theme of federal power.

Both the presidency and congress approached the problem with concern for their institutional prerogatives as well as for policies and results. Power might be exercised upon three objects: the southern states as corporate entities, in the sense of having to meet stipulations for readmission; former rebels as individuals, of whom demands could be made prior to restoration of rights; and the freedmen, who might be expected to qualify in various ways for citizenship or other political rights. The numerous possible subjects for federal action included such economic issues as land for the freedmen and repudiation of the Confederate debt; the political issues of amnesty, the franchise, and office holding; and the social position of blacks in a new South. As sources of power, the Constitution and federal statutes ranked first, though some protagonists would cite also the Declaration of Independence and even the general law of war and the authority of victor over vanquished. Finally, a mixture of motives shaped the positions urged. The desire for security against future insurrection; the commitment to equality for blacks; the wish for a strong national Republican party; the need to punish southerners; the desire for speedy resumption of peacetime national pursuits; the unwillingness to abandon familiar distributions of functions within the federal system; the reluctance to exert federal authority on behalf of blacks—all these motives impelled individual national leaders toward different programs of restoration.

Andrew Johnson's dispute with Congress over restoration became progressively more rancorous and divisive from 1865 through the debacle of impeachment in 1868. It embraced a number of specific issues, some continuous, some short-lived. From start to finish, however, it remained a conflict over power: who should exercise it, under what authority, against whom, upon what subjects, and for what purposes? The dispute was a classic disagreement over division of authority and proper function of government within a federal system—exactly the points of constitutional philosophy that concerned Johnson for twenty years before the war. Though many Republicans argued that the progress and conclusion of civil war had irrevocably changed the federal system, Johnson adhered to long-held constitutional views rather than entertain new power alignments.

Johnson assumed the presidency at a time of great confusion but also a time of great creative opportunity. No clear national program of restoration existed. Congress had gone out of session on March 4, and its most recent attempt at a step by step program, the Wade-Davis Bill of 1864, had earned a pocket veto from Lincoln. Lincoln's own 10 percent scheme had defects, as he himself knew, yet in the last public speech of his life, on the evening of April 11, he had urged acceptance of the Louisiana government, imperfect as it was. Significantly, however, he did not call his 10 percent plan the only acceptable postwar arrangement. Lincoln died hoping that he had committed the nation to a generous and fair peace and a speedy restoration but without specifying a final mechanism for achieving those goals.

Johnson assumed office with a mixed record on the issues at hand. He had agreed with Lincoln on emancipation, though certainly under his own circumstances in Tennessee. His wartime reputation for being arbitrary he justified by the need to crush secession and win the war, but Lincoln had not criticized him for it. The press still repeated his well-known hope that treason would be made odious and traitors punished and impoverished, and some of the extremists among the congressional Republicans, like Ohio's Senator Ben Wade, hoped that Johnson would cooperate with them.

Yet Johnson's philosophy was far more complex than these initial Republican hopes required, and before long it appeared that he had made a complete turnabout from scourge to friend of traitors. He had not, but the continued dominance of long-set positions served to limit his freedom of action. Like many Americans, especially of his own social and economic background, Johnson did not believe that emancipation meant full equality for blacks. He thought blacks inferior but also denounced slavery as a system of human bondage; he especially attacked slavery as an economic system, yet found it impossible for the federal government to help alleviate the economic aftermath for blacks. Since he and other whites of his class had triumphed over their origins without federal aid, so must blacks. Without question he hoped for a better southern attitude and response to his initial efforts than he received, and when it was not forthcoming in 1865, two elements of his constitutional philosophy produced a stalemate: his cherished perception of a strong executive clashed with his equally cherished but higher ranking position of the states rights approach to federal functions. The tension between the two elements continued, and the process whereby Congress settled the question of federal functions left Johnson regarding himself as the defender of an embattled presidency.

Political uncertainty added to both the confusion and the opportunity of the late spring and early summer of 1865. The war had set up some strange alignments in political parties which the assassination left even stranger. The chief executive must also be the chief of his party. But the "party" responsible for putting Johnson so close to the presidency was a coalition of Republicans and War Democrats that symbolized its hybrid nature by Johnson's presence on the ticket and the name "Union-Republican." Now, however, the antislavery sentiments that had generated and nourished the Republicans in the 1850s had come to fruition; the standards of the Union, which alone had called a coalition into existence, had come victorious through the trial; and fate had left the leadership of the "party" in the hands of the man whose lifelong membership in the historic opposition had qualified him for the coalition to begin with. Republicans pondered and Democrats chortled. Either the coalition would dissolve completely, leaving Johnson in an anomalous position, or it would continue or be reconstituted in some form or other under his personal leadership. Much that occurred in the first eighteen months of Johnson's term occurred at least in part because of party considerations. At the end of the road ahead lay the potential of either a remarkable success or a remarkable failure.

Party concerns appeared regularly in Johnson's incoming mail during the formative months of April and May 1865. Democrats hoped for positions, Republicans hoped to keep theirs, everyone expressed good wishes, and of course everyone gave advice, which varied from forgive-if-not-forget to demands for Jeff Davis's neck in a noose. Johnson sincerely appreciated these greetings, particularly when they came from the common people. From them he enjoyed praise throughout his life; from others it had less value.

Johnson was by nature a more solitary decision maker than Lincoln, and this habit increased public speculation. He kept Lincoln's cabinet, in which Secretary of State Seward, still recovering from his own near assassination, was the leader and

Johnson's chief link to the mainstream of the Republican party. Everyone watched the comings and goings at Johnson's office; if the old Democratic Blair clan and their hangers-on turned up too frequently, Republicans got skittish, whereas the presence of too many friends of Seward and his New York lieutenant, Thurlow Weed, raised Democratic fears. Congressional leaders, hopeful of maintaining institutional prerogatives and a bit resentful of the natural tendency of a four-year military crisis to focus leadership in an executive officer, hoped Johnson would call a special session rather than wait for the normal December meeting. It would have been out of character for Johnson, long an advocate though not a successful practitioner of executive hegemony, to call one, warranted or not. Instead he developed, with much personal attention and the advice of his cabinet, a program of restoration under executive authority and announced it in two proclamations on May 29.

The Amnesty Proclamation, which Johnson regarded as a derivative of Lincoln's measures of December 8, 1863 and March 26, 1864, granted full amnesty and pardon for participation in the rebellion to all Confederates except members of certain specifically excluded groups, provided the person took an oath of future loyalty to the United States and promised to support all wartime measures regarding emancipation. The excluded groups consisted largely of high-ranking civil, military, and diplomatic officials and those who had joined the rebellion after deserting federal offices of honor and trust. Most significant, however, was the thirteenth exception: "All persons who have voluntarily participated in said rebellion and the estimated value of whose taxable property is over $20,000." Johnson, long at odds with the planter class, believed that the "bobtailed aristocracy" had railroaded the "wool-hat boys" into secession without a fair chance to express an honest opinion. The provision provoked some discussion because a fragment of an original draft, possibly prepared by Attorney General James Speed, set the estimated worth figure at only $10,000.

The apparent barriers raised by the exceptions were not permanent, however. Those excluded could make special application to the President for pardon. Johnson promised to do in such cases whatever the "peace and dignity" of the country permitted. Johnson's critics thought the resulting scene quite undignified indeed, as hundreds of rebels appealed to the Presidents, some in person, some by agents, and many by fulsome essays promising loyalty and remarking on the personal qualities of the tailor-statesman. Johnson spent a great deal of time during 1865 with these cases, to the annoyance of officials who had pressing business. Possibly he got some personal satisfaction from reading the entreaties of the once powerful, but there are better explanations for his painstaking approach. Attention to detail was part of his style, and he regarded pardons as a specific executive function. He had lavished great effort on pardons during both governorships. Moreover, in 1864, nearly a year before his own presidency, he urged Lincoln to preserve the value of pardons by ending blanket grants and requiring a personal application in every case.

One provision of the Amnesty Proclamation, added during debate, particularly disappointed people like Thaddeus Stevens, who favored extensive confiscation of rebel property, and other Republicans who hoped to see ex-slaves given land. To avoid significant legal complexities, the pardon carried with it restoration of all property except slaves and property sold following legal process under one of the wartime confiscation acts.

The other May 29 proclamation established a provisional government for North Carolina in a form that then became a model for Mississippi, Georgia, Texas, Alabama, South Carolina, and Florida, whose governments Johnson created between mid-June and Mid-July. Virginia, Tennessee, Arkansas, and Louisiana continued with the governments established before the surrender. Discussion of this very topic, particularly as to North Carolina, had taken place at Lincoln's last cabinet meeting on the day of his assassination, and under

Johnson an extensive discussion picked up where it had left off with consideration of a draft Secretary of War Stanton had prepared.

Johnson appointed William Holden provisional governor of the state and assigned him broad powers to arrange an election for a state convention and, in general, to do everything "necessary and proper" to enable North Carolina to resume its "constitutional relations to the Federal Government" and to establish a "republican form of State government." The Union army would remain to assist the governor. Although the proclamation did not spell out the whole process, the state constitutional convention was the first step, which would lead to the election of a legislature, a regular governor, and members of Congress.

However, the proclamation did specifically regulate participation in the process. Only "loyal" people, meaning those who had taken the oath of May 29, could vote for the convention or be a delegate. Some presidential confidants believed that the word *loyal* had its origin in a meeting on Sunday evening, April 16, between Stanton and several Republican members of Congress, as a means of opening the door to black suffrage. If so, it failed, because the proclamation allowed the laws of North Carolina, as they existed on the eve of secession, to control other qualifications for voting. The convention, when it met, could set future qualifications for voting and officeholding under state law, or else leave the matter to the new state legislature. In a passage that was vintage Johnson, the proclamation declared this attribute of self-government "a power the people of the several States composing the Federal Union have rightfully exercised from the origin of the Government to the present time."

As of "the present time" southern states (and all but six northern ones, for that matter) restricted the franchise to whites. In the Cabinet meeting of May 9, the presidential advisers divided evenly, Stanton, Speed, and Postmaster General William Dennison favoring Negro suffrage, while Navy Secretary Gideon Welles, Treasury Secretary Hugh McCulloch, and

Interior Secretary John P. Usher opposed it. Black voting would have required positive federal action, and Johnson, always a states-righter on questions not directly related to secession, refused.

During the summer Johnson advised the South to make concessions by voluntarily extending suffrage to a limited number of blacks based on literacy, property ownership, and service in the Union army. This advice had strong political overtones, as when Johnson in August told the provisional governor of Mississippi that such a move would be a bit of oneupmanship on the "radicals," who according to Johnson were "wild" for black suffrage. In common with many Americans, however, Johnson did not believe in the general ability of blacks to participate in government, and when southern states proved resistant to his advice, he did not press the matter.

To Johnson the constitutional grounding of the North Carolina proclamation bore special importance. As a senator he had cosponsored the original war aims resolutions of 1861, which expressed the intention of quashing secession but disavowed an intention of remaking the South's domestic institutions. The North Carolina proclamation therefore had to match the government's position on the nature of the war, and it had to leave no doubt regarding the validity of the government's postsurrender policies. As the constitutional sources of his authority, Johnson cited his role as commander-in-chief of the army and navy, his position as chief of the executive branch, and his oath to see to the faithful execution of the laws. The overall source of authority for federal action was the guaranty clause, as it had been during wartime reconstruction. Johnson's philosophy was clear. Secession had initiated a civil war in the form of unlawful resistance to the federal government. The "revolutionary progress" of that rebellion had deprived the people of "all civil government" and hence of the "republican form" of government which the Constitution guaranteed them. Johnson's postwar program thus rested on the same constitutional foundation as Lincoln's wartime 10-

percent plan, though it contained no such mathematical formula and differed in other small details.

The North Carolina proclamation and its successors for other states left a number of expectations hanging, however. The states had received authority to proceed rather than a complete plan with specific requirements and promises. One question loomed large during the rest of 1865. In its southern formulation: "What is the least we shall have to do in order to regain admission to Congress?" Or as a northern Republican would have put it: "What will the President expect of the South in pledges of security to the Union and fairness to the Negro before he will ask Congress to readmit these states?"

Presidential expectations became clearer as the provisional governors carried out their functions, aided by early presidential interviews and subsequent correspondence. Each state should abrogate its ordinance of secession, recognize the end of slavery by appropriate alterations in the state constitution and by ratification of the Thirteenth Amendment (then pending since its passage by Congress in February 1865), and repudiate its Confederate war debt.

Some of the states, most notably Mississippi, performed these tasks only grudgingly. They chose to "repeal" their secession ordinances rather than declare them "null and void," thus leaving adrift the question of original validity. Some states tinkered with the language on slavery, choosing to "recognize" that it had been terminated "by force of arms" or ratifying the amendment with "reservations" about the meaning of the enforcement clause. Repudiation of the Confederate debt barely passed in Georgia and elsewhere. These little quibbles made southerners chuckle and Johnson despair. In effect the South was on probation for the last eight months of 1865, and what it did and how it acted determined northern opinion on readmission as well as on the success of Johnson's course of action.

More serious than these signs of rhetorical intransigence were two patterns that northern Republicans found particularly alarming. Prominent Confederates, frequently military figures and almost all Democrats except for a few ex-Whigs, elected to Congress might combine with northern Democrats to make the Republicans a national minority party once more. Furthermore, these people could not take the "iron-clad" oath of 1862, prescribed by Congress for all federal officeholders, which required the person to swear that he had not voluntarily borne arms against the United States. Johnson urged against the election of such men, but the South once more ignored his advice.

In addition, the legislatures that began meeting in the fall enacted Black Codes designed to limit the civil rights of blacks and restrict their economic and political opportunities. Republicans, not united on the desire for black suffrage, did agree that freedmen deserved protection; thus, they viewed restrictive southern tendencies with increasing concern and looked for signs of a similar presidential awareness.

Johnson, however, did not encourage hope. On some things he would press the South and on others he would not, and the constitutional line was quite clear. Southern states must recognize the government's right to put down secession. Confederate war debts, incurred in aid of rebellion, could not stand. As for slavery, the war had destroyed it, in practice by the fact of victory and in law by presidential action seconded by Congress and now pending state ratification. No other outcome was even thinkable. The future status of the blacks, however, was another question. Voting qualifications had always been a state matter, and Johnson did not believe that the war had given the federal government any additional authority in this area; neither had the war authorized the federal government to preempt the traditional state concerns such as ownership of property, service on juries, competency to testify, or punishment for crime. In his view, neither black voting nor protection of black civil rights was necessary to a "republican form of government." (Indeed, if they had been, there would have been serious question about the republican quality of many prewar governments both North and South.) As a consequence, Johnson found neither constitutional warrant nor war-born necessity nor personal inclination to push the South on these points.

The uncertain party situation also influenced the extent of Johnson's executive prodding. Now that the war was over, Democrats opposed further coercion of the South, and some of Johnson's closest confidants, such as the Blairs, had a well-known antipathy toward blacks. If Johnson had any desire at all for an elected presidential term of his own, in spite of his silence thus far, his only opportunity lay in either a strong, rejuvenated national Democratic party or a new coalition committed to him personally. In either case he could hardly ignore Democrats, and he kept his fences mended.

Yet Johnson had to walk a tightrope, and on two issues of interest to the Democrats he held back. Democrats hoped that military trials in the South would quickly end. Lincoln had suspended the privilege of the writ of *habeas corpus* throughout the country for war-related offenses in September 1863, and Johnson, at least for the time being, took no action to countermand that decree. The South thus remained under a limited form of martial law enforced by an occupying federal army, and Johnson often had to decide conflicts of authority between commanding generals and civilian officials. Frequently he supported the army. Furthermore, Democrats had long wanted Seward and Stanton out of the Cabinet, and although Johnson seemed to agree with their complaints, he took no action. Stanton he never particularly liked but tolerated for the time being; the more congenial Seward, back at work by July, lent stature to the Cabinet and did yeoman service in the autumn elections in New York by keeping conservative and moderate Republicans aligned with the President.

The New York elections also showed presidential cleverness. In a state in which patronage was especially important, Johnson in August appointed Preston King, a Republican with extensive Democratic connections, to the prestigious station of collector of customs at New York City. King was a personal friend and close adviser to the President—"domiciled at the Executive Mansion," according to Welles—who continued to serve Johnson until in midwinter he leaped to his death in New York Harbor from the deck of the Hoboken ferryboat. Other presidential moves were equally adroit. In October, when Horace Greeley's New York *Tribune,* one of the more advanced Republican papers on racial questions, started to doubt Johnson's policies, the President planted the remark that if he were running things in Tennessee, he could support gradual enfranchisement of blacks by state action based on military service, literacy, and property holding. Since Johnson did not personally endorse candidates, he made no enemies, and even after the Republicans won, Seward and Weed held out olive branches to the Democrats.

In New York as elsewhere in the North, Johnson had enjoyed one particular advantage for eight months: the absence of a large, organized, vocal opposition. The small number of Republicans whose hostility to the South and whose championing of black suffrage gained them the description of "radical," such as Wendell Phillips, Charles Sumner, Thaddeus Stevens, Benjamin Wade, and others, already doubted by midsummer that Johnson would support their views. Nor was this for want of their trying, either. Chief Justice Salmon Chase, an ardent devotee of Negro suffrage, whose donning of the judicial robes in 1864 scarcely covered the politician, went on an inspection tour of the South for the President and filled the mail with assurances that conditions in Dixie were ripe for black enfranchisement. On the very first evening of Johnson's presidency Sumner looked him up at the Kirkwood House, and after raising the foreign affairs trivia that provided a plausible excuse for the visit, he kept the President listening for the better part of two hours on black voting and related matters. Johnson listened politely and said little—almost a necessity whenever Sumner was monologuing along—and the senator, who loved to be agreed with, thought he was, and left happy.

Sumner and other Republicans, not all of radical, would later accuse Johnson of betraying the party. There was, however, no deliberate deceit. Though argumentative in prepared speeches, Johnson was often reserved in official conversation,

sation, and visitors who believed that silence meant assent could well feel misled. Johnson's loyal friend Gideon Welles, who mused about the habits and foibles of nearly everyone and mixed arraignment with fatherly sighs, gently chided Johnson (in his diary, at least) for this trait, which led to serious misunderstandings throughout the crucial years of 1865 and 1866. Some people caught on fast, however, and one month to the day after Lincoln's assassination Stevens clamored to Sumner: "Is there no way to avert the insane course of the President on reorganization?"

Such views were not yet dominant. Within the mainstream of both parties an extensive reservoir of good will existed even though Republicans and Democrats disagreed on specific proposals regarding military power, officeholding, property rights, and the Negro. The press as a whole reflected this sympathetic approach. Of course, each party still claimed Johnson because he had not yet given a clear indication of deserting either one. In addition to framing his policy in general terms, he had also pursued a much more restrained executive style than his earlier personal history might have indicated. His attention to duty and his self-imposed burden of pardon papers accounted for part of it, but there were other influences. Tennessee was a limited stage by comparison with Washington, where the dangers of misstep loomed greater. Also, the experience of building a personal following in Tennessee bore only limited application to the national scene because the constituent parts, even in faction-ridden Tennessee, were more homogeneous than those of a national coalition could be. In addition, the absence of Congress spared Johnson the necessity of responding to legislative actions and thus reduced the occasions for specific conflict.

Indeed, in an increasingly stormy presidency the summer and fall of 1865 must have seemed, upon reflection, while hardly inactive, yet to have been particularly tranquil. Political and personal concerns gradually came into harmony. After finally getting possession of the White House on June 9— Mary Todd Lincoln, poor woman, could hardly bear the thought of leaving—Johnson plunged headlong into his work and for a month never set foot outside the gates. His various illnesses, among which kidney stones at the moment pained their way to greatest attention, kept the doctors busy, and he gave every evidence of going the way of the last Tennesseean to be there, James K. Polk, who worked himself into an early grave. But Gideon Welles, with all the resources of the Navy at his command, soon came to the rescue, and little boat trips on the Potomac helped. Then the presidential family—all eleven of them, counting the Pattersons and the Stovers— arrived, and a definite lightening of mood occurred. Eliza's contribution was more spritual than managerial since advancing weakness confined her to the second floor, while daughter Martha acted as hostess. The various grandchildren, if not quite so rowdy as the Theodore Roosevelt brood, invited their playmates to snack with the President, and Preston King, a portly man with whiting hair and a rumpled appearance, often regaled the juvenile lunch table with tales of Jolly Roger and Captain Kidd. Frequent expeditions to Rock Creek Park involved pony riding, rock chunkin', wildflower gathering, and other youthful diversions. Johnson found time to meditate during these outings and reflected upon how long his presidential independence would last. Lincoln had said once or twice before his assassination that he was glad Congress was out of session, and certainly Johnson made use of the opportunity.

Constitutional calendars have their imperatives, however, and after the summer of executive hegemony came the winters of reckoning and of legislative discontent. What Johnson had proclaimed in May he must explain in December, and so he began preparing his annual message for Congress. To draft it he commissioned prestigious George Bancroft, a strong Jacksonian Democrat whose career as a historian gave him an elegance with language. This former member of Polk's cabinet assumed an increasingly important role as a presidential correspondent during the summer and provided continuity of moderate counsel after the suicide of King. While Bancroft drafted the message at home in New York, the President sent him material and ideas—a quote from Jefferson, a passage from Charles James Fox—and though the style was Bancroft's, the substance was clearly Johnson's.

In tone the message was mild and moderate. It described what Johnson had initiated in the South, what had occurred, and the philosophy behind it. For the future, Johnson hoped for a speedy resumption of normal relations. He clearly referred two specific questions—judgment on the qualifications of members-elect and the reopening of federal courts in Virginia—to Congress without either inviting a general participation in the work of Reconstruction or warning against encroachment on a presumed presidential sphere of authority.

Johnson's constitutional picture of a national government with ample power to defend itself and states with domestic areas of competence unaffected by the war stood clearly revealed. Ultimate power resided in the people, which meant that government at all levels had to respect the idea that "the American system rests on the assertion of the equal right of every man to life, liberty, and the pursuit of happiness, to freedom of conscience, to the culture and exercise of all his faculties." Slavery, a prime cause of prior discord, Johnson had opposed as a monopoly of labor; its abolition the South must recognize by constitutional process. The South also had to give "evidence of sincerity in the future maintenance of the Union," while the North allowed the plan of restoration to go forward "in conformity with a willingness to cast the disorders of the past into oblivion."

As for "the plan of restoration," military government would not have "restored affection" but would have "envenomed hatred" by its divisive character, inability to suppress discontent, great expense, large-scale addition to federal patronage, and likelihood of long duration once established. His own program needed "at least the acquiescence" of the southern states and also implied "an invitation to those States, by renewing their allegiance to the United States, to resume their functions as States of the Union." He admitted the risk but called it necessary and, "in the choice of difficulties," the "smallest" risk.

For many readers the crucial passages dealt with the freedmen. Johnson made it clear that neither he nor Congress could force Negro suffrage on the states by anything in the Constitution or wartime enactments. "Good faith" required protection of blacks in their life, liberty, and property, but a vagueness about federal power on the subject reinforced a clear preference that the states undertake the task. Both management and labor, he thought, had substantial economic self-interest in fairness and justice.

The attention directed to general domestic matters reflected Johnson's long-standing points of view: support for unrestricted commerce; a reflection on the benefits of the homestead policy; a desire to reduce military expenses; a cautious fiscal policy and sound currency; a tax system that burdened luxuries more than necessities; and a reduction of the national debt. After descriptions of the greatness of America reminiscent of the annual messages of the fifties came a concluding prayer for divine guidance in passing on the virtues of the constitutional system "to our posterity, and they to theirs through countless generations." Yet prayer could not solve the dilemmas of Reconstruction, in whose tangled politics the trinity of faith, hope, and charity clashed with a fourth discordant element, and that was power.

VIII

First Clashes with Congress
1865–1866

HAD NOT Thomas Jefferson been such a weak-voiced individual, there might never have developed the 112-year tradition, broken finally by preachy ex-college professor Woodrow Wilson, that presidents sent their annual messages to Congress rather than read them in person. Though Andrew Johnson had a fine, strong, melodious voice and might have enjoyed the prospect of addressing a joint session of Congress, he followed the prevailing practice and sent his message, which clerks read in each house separately on Tuesday, December 5, 1865. Monday saw the chambers organize themselves for business, a process that on this occasion bore significance far beyond the purely ministerial. First, as the clerks called the offical rolls in each house, they omitted the names of persons elected from the erstwhile Confederacy and the names of those states as well. This procedure, already discussed publicly in the press and privately in the Republican caucus, took no one by surprise.

Second, Congress accepted Stevens's idea for a joint committee of both houses on reconstruction to "inquire into the condition" of the South and to report whether those states "were entitled to be represented" in Congress. Pending final action on this committee's report, neither house would seat any delegate from a seceded state. The vote of 133 to 36 indicated overwhelming support from all shades of Republican opinion, including many who sincerely believed that they were voting for institutional freedom of action rather than against Andrew Johnson.

The President, however, saw the opening scenes very differently and much out of harmony with his view of the constitutional nature of the war. Saying that the states were not *entitled* to be represented was to him the same as admitting that secession had in fact taken them out of the Union. He asserted consistently during the war that the loyal people of a Confederate state had the right to be represented in Congress by a loyal delegate. He himself personified that condition in the case of Tennessee, and he remembered that Tennessee, Virginia, and Louisiana had all been represented at one time or another during the war by men elected and seated after their states had seceded. Loyalty was for him the proper test, whether during the war or after. By that test, disloyal southern senators—and even a disloyal Indianan, too, with Johnson's excoriation ringing in his ears—had been expelled. Now, by the same test, surely one could distinguish between, on the one hand, Joseph Fowler and his own son-in-law David Patterson of Tennessee and, on the other, rebel ex-Vice-President Alexander Stephens, senator-elect of Georgia. Johnson recognized that each house had the right to judge the qualifications of its own members but denied that this authority permitted refusal of a state's right to representation at all. Congress, however, was more interested in the condition of the South generally than in individual cases.

The President's message was so lacking in specifics about southern conditions and so filled with hopeful moderation about policy that newspapers of very different political leanings praised it. Democratic papers thought it presaged the end of military occupation and a limit to federal involvement in matters of race and other domestic questions; Republican editors said that because it left room for congressional action and favored protection for blacks, Johnson would not desert the party or fight with Congress.

Clearly the President hoped to keep the support of the political center. Extremist Republicans like Charles Sumner and "Copperhead" Democrats like Clement Vallandigham, the latter tried by wartime military commission for disloyalty, held no appeal for Johnson. Yet the politics of the center involved hazards. The effort to harmonize the interests of disparate groups in both parties incurred a complex set of expectations. The trouble was that in late 1865 the executive and legislative branches had expectations of each other that by mid-1866 proved mutually unacceptable.

Not long after Congress convened, presidential friends and critics alike asked for more details on southern conditions. Johnson sent two reports by prominent generals. Carl Schurz, who toured from South Carolina to Louisiana between July and October, noted that governmental machinery was once again functioning but that popular loyalty amounted to nothing more than "submission to necessity" and that the freedmen required "a certain measure of political power" to protect themselves from "class legislation" and "private persecution." Ulysses Grant, after a much shorter tour in November, recommended temporary continuation of a military force in Dixie but generally found southerners to be "in earnest in wishing to do what they think is required by the government, not humiliating to them as citizens, and that if such a course were pointed out they would pursue it in good faith."

Johnson added a few paragraphs of his own, asserting that except for "occasional disorders" of a "local" nature, southerners were recognizing federal authority "with more willingness and greater promptitude than under the circumstances could reasonably have been anticipated." He observed that "systems are gradually developing themselves under which the freedman will receive the protection to which he is justly entitled, and, by means of his labor, make himself a useful and independent member in the community in which he has a home." The word *systems* offered an oblique assertion that the Black Codes, with their provisions on vagrancy and labor contracts, would sufficiently answer the needs of economic reorganization.

The Joint Committee on Reconstruction did not tour the South, but it did amass a great deal of testimony in hearings. Though heavily Republican in composition, the committee contained few radicals; Stevens was there, but the Senate kept the anxious Sumner off, and appointed instead moderates like James Grimes and William Pitt Fessenden, the latter of whom became chairman. Democrats criticized the committee for its excessive selectivity of witnesses and highly leading questions —a fair assessment—but even so, the committee assembled much evidence of maltreatment of blacks and lack of devotion to the Union. The longer the committee investigated, the clearer it became that the South had not cooperated with Johnson in the proper spirit and that for his generosity, defiance had been his portion. Increasingly his annual message seemed like a simplistic gloss, and his comments with the two reports a blind effort to paint success where failure's dark colors dominated the canvas.

Congress contemplated a legislative solution for these deficiencies, but the process took time; not until the second week in February did the first Reconstruction measure reach Johnson's desk. In the meantime, everyone scanned press reports of presidential interviews for clues to his intentions. Just before the Christmas recess two Iowa congressmen, James F. Wilson and Hiram Price, told him that the congressional majority would "expect and ask" that Johnson not interfere with a legislative program "by the distribution of partonage or in any other way." Otherwise "serious opposition" would result; things would be a lot better if each branch "simply leaves the other to do what it considers its duty." Johnson always prided himself on doing his duty as he saw it, but Wilson's formula for avoiding trouble was not a workable one in the context either of the times or the structure of the federal government.

In spite of the implied threat he merely replied that he hoped to avoid a conflict and said nothing about interference.

To visitors from Montana Territory on February 7 he observed: "The sand of my political glass has well-nigh run out." Since his ambition would be "filled, and filled to overflowing" when the Union was restored, he said, "I feel that I can afford to do right, and so feeling, God being willing, I intend to do right, and so far as in me lies I intend to administer this Government upon the principles that lie at the foundation of it." If true, this denial of future political ambition would provide a simple explanation for the single-mindedness of Johnson's later fateful actions. There were, however, personal and philosophical explanations of long standing for his course, and in any event Johnson was hardly the man to deny the people a chance to return him to the office he had long sought.

On the same day, he told a group of northern and southern blacks, including Frederick Douglass, that the franchise would do blacks more harm than good. Blacks, he said, had come out of the war free and thus had gained much, but loyal, non-slaveholding whites had been forced into the war and had often come out without what little estate they once owned. The two should certainly not "be thrown together at the ballot-box with this enmity and hate existing between them. The query arises, if, there, we don't commence a war of races." If blacks could not prosper in the South without the franchise, Johnson added, let them emigrate.

This meeting clearly irritated Johnson. Douglass had not only asked for the ballot, but he had been disposed to debate and found fault with Johnson's "fundamental tenet" of obeying popular will as expressed at the ballotbox. He may have struck Johnson as a black version of Charles Sumner because the President observed that "my means, my time, my all has been perilled" for the blacks and added, "I am free to say to you that I do not like to be arraigned by some who can get up handsomely rounded periods and deal in rhetoric, and talk about abstract ideas of liberty, who never perilled life, liberty, or property." After they left, Johnson used more earthy language to his private secretary: "Those damned sons of bitches thought they had me in a trap! I know that damned Douglass; he's just like any nigger, and he would sooner cut a white man's throat than not."

Douglass had said that Johnson had the power "to bless or blast us," and many people would conclude that presidential actions during the next six weeks showed a disposition toward the latter course. On February 14 Johnson received the first piece of Reconstruction legislation and the first to deal with the blacks. It extended the lifetime and the jurisdiction of the Bureau of Refugees, Freedmen, and Abandoned Lands, a War Department agency headed by General Oliver O. Howard. Congress had created it in the spring of 1865 to assist blacks in making the transition to social and economic self-support. Its areas of concern included education, marriage, labor contracts, and disputes between blacks and their white employers. Originally chartered to operate for a year after formal declaration of the rebellion's end, it now had an indefinite life, a strengthened system of quasi-military courts to enforce its decrees, and the authority to function anywhere in the country where freedmen needed its protection.

On February 19, after a special three-hour meeting of the Cabinet, Johnson returned the bill with a veto. He called the measure unnecessary; the absence of a formal declaration of peace meant that the original law still had a year or longer to run. He also objected to punishing under military authority whites who violated the "civil rights and immunities" of blacks, with no specification of what those rights and immunities were and without the procedural safeguards of the Bill of Rights. "Undoubtedly the freedman should be protected," he said, "but he should be protected by the civil authorities, especially by the exercise of all the constitutional powers of the courts of the United States and of the States."

Johnson complained that, for the benefit of blacks, the bill took land from former owners without legal process and that it authorized Congress to spend money on blacks in ways never considered proper for whites—rental or purchase of homes, establishment of asylums for the helpless, development of schools. "A system for the support of indigent persons in the United States was never contemplated by the authors of the Constitution," he observed, "nor can any good reason be advanced why, as a permanent establishment, it should be founded for one class or color of our people more than another."

This was Andrew Johnson the author of the Homestead Act. Such objections were hardly surprising on the part of a man who had always believed in the virtues of hard work and self-support and who had unbounded confidence that honest effort, being good, would in the end triumph over economic elitism, being bad. His own life had acted out the drama; his speeches constantly repeated the story. And he clearly believed that blacks had a number of ecomomic factors in their favor, most notably the law of supply and demand. Since black labor was indispensable, the freedman should be able to "command almost his own terms," and if unsuccessful in one place, he could move to a better one. "It is no more than justice to them," he observed, "to believe that as they have received their freedom with moderation and forbearance, so they will distinguish themselves by their industry and thrift, and soon show the world that in a condition of freedom they are self-sustaining, capable of selecting their own employment and their own places of abode, of insisting for themselves on a proper remuneration, and of establishing and maintaining their own asylums and schools."

Johnson also knew, though he did not mention, that Congress had under consideration a bill to extend the 1862 Homestead Act to the public land states of the South: Alabama, Mississippi, Florida, Arkansas, and Louisiana. Not only did it exclude rebels and specifically prohibit discrimination against blacks (the 1862 law contained a citizenship clause), but on February 5 Indiana radical George W. Julian said in debate that it was needed to provide homes for both poor whites and Negroes. When the measure reached Johnson in June, he signed it.

Republicans, however, in combating the Freedmen's veto,

would point to increasing evidence that Johnson's estimate of southern conditions was very wrong and that planters still had both an opportunity and a desire to exploit laborers. But the President would not sway from the beliefs of a lifetime. Clearly not a spokesman for political equality for blacks, he was nonetheless a spokesman for a different sort of equality—equality of expectations—in that he judged blacks, whether unrealistically or not, by the same standards he had always applied to white yeoman farmers and mechanics. "Any legislation that shall imply that they are not expected to attain a self-sustaining condition must have a tendency injurious alike to their character and their prospects."

Aside from criticizing specific provisions of the bill, Johnson for the first time during Reconstruction laid the foundation for a strong institutional position: "The President of the United States stands toward the country in a somewhat different attitude from that of any member of Congress. Each member of Congress is chosen from a single district or State; the President is chosen by the people of all the States." Until the South returned, "it would seem to be his duty on all proper occasions to present their just claims to Congress." For the moment, he contented himself with recommending the admission of people whose loyalty "can not be questioned under any existing constitutional or legal test" and added that "most of those States, so far, at least, as depends upon their own actions" were restored and entitled to recognition.

In preparing this message, Johnson conferred regularly with individual members of the Cabinet and solicited ideas in writing, from which he borrowed and expanded. Seward approved the veto, though the message was sharper on a number of points than his own draft; McCulloch, Welles, and Dennison also supported the President. Stanton, Speed, and James Harlan, new to the Interior post, "while they did not dissent, evidently regretted that the President had not signed the bill," according to Welles. Some of Johnson's views clearly reflected Grant's report of his November sojourn in the South. The general, although he called the Bureau "in some form" an "absolute necessity" for a time, criticized it for mismanagement and failure to disabuse blacks of the notion "that a freed-man has the right to live without care or provision for his future." Johnson also had to consider the party alignments. No Democrats in either house voted for the bill, and the presidential mail sacks brought calls for action from Democrats in increased numbers. The general lines of the message agreed with Democratic positions, and Republicans could well see in the veto the strongest sign yet that Johnson's views differed from theirs.

Indeed, there was more than a difference, for Johnson showed an increasing tendency to categorize Republicans as pro- and antiadministration and to assume that radicals were more numerous than they were. In that view he misread certain important political circumstances. The bill was not the product of radicals and had heavy support throughout the Republican party except for a few conservatives like Senators James Dixon and James Doolittle. Moreover, its author, Illinois Senator Lyman Trumbull, who was not even a member of the Reconstruction Committee, thought he had obtained Johnson's support before the bill passed, although this proved to be a case of Trumbull hearing what he wanted to hear in noncommittal presidential conversations. Any president, of course, can use a veto to test his support, but in this case the instrument ill served the purpose. Not only was it unlikely to cut the true extremists out of the Republican herd and bring the rest into his camp, but in fact his friends in the Senate sustained it only with difficulty. Johnson clearly picked up Democratic support, but now there remained few moderate Republicans for an alliance. He had weakened his leadership in important quarters by vetoing a law widely regarded as moderate and necessary. Yet his reasons for vetoing it fully coincided with long-held views on power relationships within a federal system.

Republicans alienated by Johnson's policy shortly found themselves further alienated by his style. On Washington's birthday, three days after the veto, he gave an impromptu speech to a group of citizens who serenaded him at the White House. He charged abolitionists and secessionists with equal guilt for disunion: "One would destroy the government to preserve slavery; the other would break up the government to destroy slavery." Stevens, Sumner, and Phillips were "opposed to the fundamental principles of this government" and "now laboring to destory them." He accused the trio of being responsible, through their extremist and disunionist agitation, for the death of Lincoln. If he too should be marked for death, he added, "let an altar of the Union be erected, and then if necessary lay me upon it, and the blood that now warms and animates my frame shall be poured out in a last libation as a tribute to the Union; and let the opponents of this government remember that when it is poured out the blood of the martyr will be the seed of the church."

To sort out allegory from actuality in all this was virtually impossible. The press circulated the speech widely in one version or another, and some editors rumored that he was again raving drunk, an unlikely circumstance. Welles told Johnson he should not have "permitted himself to be drawn into giving names of those whose course he disapproved." Coming on the heels of the Freedmen's Bureau veto, this speech made Johnson seem reckless and violent, and in truth he was more prone to talk privately about conspiracies and to adopt a "me-against-them" outlook than he had been even three months earlier.

Yet Johnson could also be lucid and moderate, as in an interview with Ohio Governor Jacob D. Cox, published on February 27. Since Johnson had come to office in the absence of any congressional policy at all, he had modeled one on Lincoln's views. He favored "the admission of the freedmen to various rights, &c," but he intended to encourage the South to do the right thing by itself. Cox raised the possibility that Congress could legislate civil protection in federal courts for blacks in states that refused to do so. This Johnson considered to be "exactly parallel" to his own thoughts, but he offered no specific plan to accomplish it because if the South took the proper steps, "nothing further on our part would be necessary. If they did not do what they ought, there would then be time to elaborate a plan."

Congress increasingly doubted that the South would "do what they ought," and prepared more legislation to remedy the matter. In March, the second major postwar statute reached Johnson's desk. The Civil Rights Bill established the first definition of citizenship in federal law by declaring "all persons born or naturalized in the United States and not subject to any foreign power, excluding Indians not taxed" to be United States citizens. It then gave citizens, regardless of race, color, or previous condition of servitude, the same rights of making and enforcing contracts, bringing suit, giving testimony, and engaging in property transactions that whites enjoyed. It decreed "full and equal benefits of all laws and proceedings for the security of person and property" and forbade different punishment for the two races, "any law, statute, ordinance, regulation, or custom, to the contrary notwithstanding." Additional sections provided for federal punishment of "any person," which in practice meant any state or local official, who deprived an "inhabitant" of any right guaranteed by the act, and allowed persons who could not enforce in state courts a right guaranteed by the act to transfer their cases, either civil or criminal, to federal courts. Extensive procedural sections completed the measure.

Since the Civil Rights Bill provided for civil remedies, it seemed to meet Johnson's chief objections to the military authority of the Freedmen's Bureau. It applied uniformly throughout the country, and it did specify what rights it protected. Furthermore, the definition of federal citizenship cleared up the ambiguity on that point left over from the Dred Scott case. Yet the bill did not originate from the February veto, for Lyman Trumbull had introduced it along with the Freedmen's Bureau measure in December, and he somehow believed that Johnson would not oppose either of them. Indeed, the Civil Rights Bill partially conformed to the Cox interview.

However, on March 27 the President vetoed the Civil Rights Bill. He objected to the wholesale grant of citizenship to the black race so soon after their emergence from slavery and without the period of preparation required of aliens, a feature that discriminated "against large numbers of intelligent, worthy, and patriotic foreigners." The equal-protection portion of the bill he criticized because it prevented states from determining that social policy made discrimination necessary, as "it has frequently been thought expedient" to do in matters such as intermarriage.

The heart of Johnson's objections concerned the bill's extensive intrusions on the familiar balance of constitutional power between state and federal government, as protected by a strict reading of the Tenth Amendment. Further, if Congress could negate state laws on the subjects covered by the bill, nothing would prevent it from mandating black suffrage and officeholding. The punishment of state officials for carrying out provisions of state law he also found to be of "doubtful constitutionality." The provision allowing blacks to be tried by federal courts for crimes against state law when state courts failed to treat them fairly he found to violate the Constitution's definition of the jurisdiction of federal courts.

"I do not propose to consider the policy of this bill," Johnson said as he neared the end of his message—and then he added a few thoughts, anyway. The end of slavery had destroyed the old economic relationship in which capital owned labor and set up a new one: "They stand now each master of itself." A period of "adjustment" was necessary, and if left alone, the "laws that regulate capital and labor" would "satisfactorily work out the problem." But the bill "intervenes between capital and labor and attempts to settle questions of political economy through the agency of numerous officials whose interest it will be to foment discord between the two races, for as the breach widens their employment will continue, and when it is closed their occupation will terminate." The last point reflected Johnson's belief that the bill encouraged the manufacture of cases by allowing specially appointed "commissioners" a $10 fee for each case and deputies a $5 fee for each person arrested, whether convicted or not.

"In all our history," Johnson observed, "in all our experience as a people living under Federal and State law, no such system as that contemplated by the details of this bill has ever before been proposed or adopted. They establish for the security of the colored race safeguards which go infinitely beyond any that the General Government has ever provided for the white race." Those statements were true; the next assertion, however, had less merit: "In fact, the distinction of race and color is by the bill made to operate in favor of the colored and against the white race." Once more he reiterated his main point: the bill would "sap and destroy" the traditional federal system of government.

Johnson did say that he would "cheerfully cooperate" in enacting any legislation on the subject that was both necessary and constitutional, but Congress preferred the measure it had just drafted and so passed it over the veto. Republicans who had upheld the Freedmen's Bureau veto deserted Johnson this time to provide the necessary votes. Even so, the margin in the Senate was paper thin, and had it not been for the Republican-engineered ouster of New Jersey Democrat John P. Stockton on a credentials issue, the last-minute and unexpected defection of New York's Edwin Morgan (who had visited Johnson while reflecting), and the consequent refusal of the seriously ill Dixon to go to the Capitol and vote in a lost cause, the veto would have held up.

The Cabinet would have preferred Johnson to sign the bill. Only Welles, who found it more repulsive than the Alien and Sedition Acts of 1798, registered complete opposition, though Seward found parts of it unconstitutional. The others hoped Johnson would ignore minor defects and sign. Harlan "thought it very desirable that the President and Congress should act in concert if possible."

Harmony was certainly preferable to discord, but Johnson found the price too high. This measure, like its predecessor, had clearly divided Democrats from Republicans, and to have signed it would have jeopardized the Democratic role in the new party alignments Johnson hoped to achieve. Of much greater import, however, was the constitutional aspect. In the case of the Freedmen's Bureau measure, Johnson might perhaps have stretched a point, considered it a temporary expedient, told the South to shape up, and signed the measure after several blinks on constitutional issues. But the Civil Rights Bill was an entirely different matter. He could not possibly have signed it without turning his back on the philosophy of a lifetime. Perhaps by comparison with the punitive portions of the Fourteenth Amendment (then being drafted) and the significantly increased military authority of the 1867 Reconstruction Act, and certainly by comparison with what history often records about the aftermath of unsuccessful rebellions elsewhere in the world, the Civil Rights Bill was a moderate measure. That it drew support from Republicans who opposed the extreme views of Stevens and Sumner reinforced that impression. Yet from Johnson's standpoint the bill was an extremely radical attack on federalism and the relationship between government and the individual. He was correct in asserting that the rights to be protected had always been the responsibility of the states and not the federal government, and the central issue was therefore one of constitutional assignment of power within a federal system.

From the period of his first veto onward, Johnson viewed his opponents as being all radicals, out to circumvent not only constitutional principles but himself personally and the executive department specifically. Although this estimate was exaggerated, it did have a core of truth, for ever since early 1862 indications of leniency or softness on Lincoln's part had aroused the ire of Republicans who insisted on congressional supremacy and did not hesitate to criticize the executive. Thus, by 1866 there was a clearly developed pattern of opposition to executive forms of conciliation by a minority within the Republican party that could on selected measures get support from more moderate elements. Against this background and in view of his own personal career as a twice-frustrated executive, it is hardly surprising that Johnson saw himself as the defender of an embattled presidency as well as of the Constitution and the loyal, nonslaveholding white yeomen farmers and mechanics of the South. The trouble was that he seemed to be unable to protect those interests without also defending the entire South after it had refused to cooperate with his efforts at leniency. The radicals thus regarded him as the kind of softheaded executive they had been opposing all along and certainly less palatable than the previous one.

Even so, it was not yet clear that Congress had seized control. On April 2, even before the Civil Rights override, the President issued a "peace" proclamation declaring the rebellion suppressed throughout the country except in Texas (which had not yet completed reorganization of its government). He cited a long string of wartime proclamations and other measures, particularly the 1861 war aims resolutions, and declared that since secession was quashed and federal authority restored, the state of war was at an end. Only Seward among the Cabinet had foreknowledge and even he only several hours. "A sudden determination seems to have influenced the President," said Welles. "He did not state his reasons, but it is obvious that the Radicals are taken somewhat by surprise and view it as checkmating some of their legislation."

The proclamation began the year's phaseout period for the Freedmen's Bureau under the 1865 law, and it raised questions about the legitimate extent of martial law and military arrests in the South. These functions continued; however, in subsequent cases the Supreme Court recognized that the proclamation and its August 20 supplement for Texas marked the end of the Civil War for legal purposes.

Three more laws tested the relative strength of Johnson and Congress. In May a bill proposed statehood for Colorado, and most radicals favored it even though the proposed constitution restricted voting to whites. The clear purpose of the act was to increase the antiadministration contingent in the Senate, since the population of Colorado was far below the figure warranting statehood, and Johnson's veto stuck. Then statehood for Nebraska, similarly motivated despite an identical franchise restriction, died with a pocket veto. In July, on the other hand, a new Freedmen's Bureau bill very much like the February measure went through over Johnson's objections, thus partially counteracting the effect of the April 2 proclamation.

The most important product of the Thirty-ninth Congress never required presidential action, however. Constitutional amendments go directly to the states for ratification, and on June 12 Congress adopted the Fourteenth Amendment, a synthesis of many proposals in the works ever since December 1865. Among other purposes, the amendment sought to render permanent the principles of the Civil Rights Act, for some important Republicans, notably John A. Bingham, had doubted the law's constitutionality without an amendment. Section 1 thus incorporated the citizenship and equal-protection features of the act and added guarantees of due process and of the privileges and immunities (unspecified) of federal citizenship. Section two eliminated the old three-fifths clause by basing representation on population and, as a roundabout way of encouraging Negro suffrage, threatened to reduce a state's representation in the House if it denied the vote to any adult males for reasons other than conviction of crime or participation in rebellion. Section three disqualified from federal and state office those rebels who had been officeholders before the war, but Congress could remove this disability by two-thirds vote.

Except for the Thirteenth Amendment, which he distinguished on the ground that it confirmed the end of an institution that had threatened the life of the Union, Johnson disapproved of amending the Constitution while states were unrepresented in Congress. In January he had said that if the Constitution needed any amendment, which he doubted, the best thing was to base representation on the number of male voters as qualified by the particular state, an interesting twist on section two of the amendment proposed.

Johnson did not, however, approve of the amendment

proposed, and he sent Congress a special message on June 22. Since "the sovereign people of the nation" had not yet spoken on the questions involved, he doubted whether Congress had acted "in harmony with the sentiments of the people" and whether state legislatures "elected without reference to such an issue" ought to decide upon its ratification.

Two days later Johnson had another opportunity to criticize the amendment. The Tennessee legislature, albeit under highly irregular circumstances, ratified it, whereupon Congress passed a joint resolution declaring the state "restored to her former proper practical relations to the Union" and eligible for representation in Congress. This resolution came to Johnson for approval. Since, as he said, he wished to eliminate all causes of delay, "whether real or imaginary, on the part of Congress," in Tennessee's readmission, he signed the measure, "notwithstanding the anomalous character of this proceeding." But he insisted that his signature did not mean assent to the claims made in the resolution, especially that states could only be restored to their "former political relations" by congressional consent. Tennessee was the only Confederate state to ratify in 1866, however, and Johnson's opposition to the amendment strengthened the resolve of other states not to accede.

The character of the amendment as a condition precedent to readmission, together with its intent to establish federal protection in areas traditionally of state concern, distressed Johnson. To a states rightist, the Fourteenth Amendment was a constitutional revolution even if it did occur through the established amending process. His complaint that the people had not spoken could be remedied, however, for the mid-term congressional elections, as well as some state contests, occurred in the fall, and Johnson, as always, was certain that the people would follow "correct principles."

Preparations for the fall canvass were extremely delicate. The President still sought to ride both the Republican and Democratic horses, an increasingly balky team. Congress never succeeded in drafting any reconstruction legislation during 1866 that enjoyed bipartisan support, for if Democrats would not support the Freedmen's Bureau measure, they would not likely support anything else. Johnson refused to press Democrats to support Republican measures; indeed, he preferred Republicans to move closer to Democratic positions, which, of course, they would not do. As a result, the inherent authority of the presidential office could not shape a solution.

The spring and summer of 1866 increased Johnson's identification with Democratic principles. In state elections he supported only candidates who approved his "general policy" and "specific measures," including not only the annual message and two vetoes but the Washington's birthday speech as well. Johnson also made more extensive use of patronage as a weapon than he had in 1865. He removed over a thousand postmasters and customs and revenue agents between August and November and said that he intended thereafter to appoint only loyal supporters.

Changes in the Cabinet, too, figured in the political maneuvering. The Democrats had long wanted Seward and Stanton out not only because both supported (in different degrees) continued use of the army in the South, but also because both had taken sides in Lincoln's cabinet against Montgomery Blair. Johnson never did satisfy the Democrats, however, for Seward, whom Johnson called an "Old Roman," remained until the end, and Stanton until his removal in February 1868 prompted the impeachment. Three other cabinet portfolios did change hands. Speed, Dennison, and Harlan were by now only weak supporters of the President. One of Johnson's private secretaries, cataloging in his diary some presidential observations on the Cabinet, noted of Harlan: "Could never look you in the face." Of Speed: "The President did not consider him of any account. His wife, the President always insisted, was the better man of the two." Dennison resigned on July 11; Speed and Harlan followed before the month was out.

On July 20 Johnson nominated Henry Stanbery of Ohio, a prominent Cincinnati lawyer, a strong Lincoln supporter, and a Republican of Whig antecedents, as Attorney General, and the Senate shortly confirmed him. During the same week Alexander Randall, a vigorous war governor of Wisconsin whose prewar allegiances had carried him from Whig to Democrat to Free Soil to Republican, took over the Postmaster General's seat. Within a month Orville Browning, an Illinois Whig-Republican who had supported some of Lincoln's policies but not emancipation, took over the Interior post Harlan had vacated. Stanbery, a college graduate at sixteen and lawyer at twenty-one, was the strongest of the new trio in intellect and presidential support, and all worked more harmoniously than their predecessors.

Yet a strong political organization required more than electoral pressure, management of patronage, and shifting of advisers, and Johnson's supporters did extensive work during the summer of 1866. On June 8 Welles and McCulloch visited Johnson for an hour. According to Welles, "We all concurred that it was not possible to go on much longer with a view of preserving the integrity of the Republican Party" because of "direct antagonism" between the executive and "Radical" party leaders in Congress, especially when congressional Democrats supported the administration more often than many Republicans did. After Congress passed the Fourteenth Amendment in mid-June, executive counterplanning stepped up.

The result of a ten-day series of presidential conferences, which at one time or another included Seward, Welles, McCulloch, Browning, Randall, Doolittle, and Pennsylvania Senator Edgar Cowan, was a call for a "national convention of friends of the Union" to meet in Philadelphia on August 14. The text of the call was a clear Johnson platform. It condemned secession and denial of representation as equally iniquitious, approved the end of slavery, upheld states' rights on domestic questions and especially the franchise, approved the war aims resolutions of 1861, and scored the "usurpation and centralization of power in Congress" as revolutionary. While it made some general references to federalism and balance of power, it did not specifically mention the Fourteenth Amendment. Johnson reluctantly agreed to the omission upon the insistence of Seward, who wished to avoid alienating as many Republicans as possible, presumably those not already alienated by references to congressional usurpation. Welles complained bitterly over omission of the amendment and believed that Johnson, "usually sagacious," had allowed Seward to bamboozle him and make the whole idea of a National Union Convention into a scheme for a "Seward party," which perforce could not be Democratic. Yet old Frank Blair approved the call, to Welles' surprise and pleasure, and on July 4 forty-one congressional Democrats joined in.

The convention met for three days amid great hoopla, which began when the Massachusetts and South Carolina delegates came down the aisle together, arms interlocked, to symbolize the end of sectional strife. Resolutions criticized the recent legislation but did not brand Congress as revolutionary, and the delegates pledged their "cordial and sincere support" to Johnson.

But if the convention handled Congress gingerly, Johnson certainly did not, and when he formally received the resolutions at the White House, he responded with a forceful extempore effort. "Having placed myself upon that broad platform [the Constitution], I have not been awed or dismayed or intimidated by either threats or encroachments, but have stood there, in conjunction with partiotic spirits, sounding the tocsin of alarm when I deemed the citadel of liberty in danger." He protested the "tyranny which the dominant party in Congress has so unrelentingly exercised." and observed, "We have seen Congress gradually encroach step by step upon constitutional rights, and violate, day after day and month after month, fundamental principles of the Government." He called the convention's resolutions a second Declaration of Independence — "Glorious!" thrilled the oft-cheering deputation — and "neither the taunts nor jeers of Congress, nor of a subsidized, calumniating press, can drive me from my purpose."

This speech was mild compared with what followed. Warming up to the challenge of a full campaign, Johnson planned a speaking tour of the North and Midwest. On this "swing around the circle," which lasted from August 28 to September 15, Johnson and a large retinue of political and military notables traveled by special train from Baltimore as far as New York, Detroit, and St. Louis. At first the crowds were either enthusiastic and friendly or else merely polite, but as the trip progressed, it became evident that the radicals wished to embarrass the President by various means, including planting hecklers in the crowds to bait him.

And the President, unfortunately, let himself be baited all too often, as for example at Cleveland on September 3. The crowd was particularly boisterous and unruly— "evidently a concerted plan" to silence or embarrass Johnson, so Welles thought—but the Tennesseean determined to get the better of them. In a very rambling and disconnected speech he accused Congress of "trying to break up the Government," referred to some of his chief opponents as "traitors," and challenged the rowdies to come out of the crowd so that the torchlight would reveal the "cowardice and treachery" in their faces. After a while the crowd let Johnson finish, but the little victories proved Pyrrhic. Welles lamented to his diary, "The President should not be a stump speaker." Of course, the President always had been a stump speaker, and his Tennessee tactics made bad copy in hostile newspapers, though how much the "swing" cost Johnson is difficult to assess numerically. He clearly had become not only more abusive but also more extreme in his analysis of the issues and more arrogantly defensive about "my policy," as the press called it.

Johnson in the autumn of 1866 offered a much more sharply defined and defiant target than in the autumn of 1865, and the voters, since they could not fire directly at him, took aim at congressional targets who supported him. The results were devastating. There would now clearly be a two-thirds majority against the President in the Fortieth Congress of 1867–69. Back in August, when Johnson was still basking in the warmth of the National Union Convention, he had said, "I acknowledge no superior except my God, the author of my existence, and the people of the United States. The commands of the one I try to obey as best I can, compatible with poor humanity. As to the other, in a political and representative sense, the high behests of the people have always been, and ever will be, respected and obeyed by me." Now in November, the behests had undesired content.

IX

A Watershed and a Belated Decision

1867

"LOOK AT Peoria!" enthused Andrew Johnson one day before the 1866 elections, when the results of a minor contest got escalated into a harbinger of good things to come. The American heartland had many Peorias, and Johnson counted on their cumulative voices to shout defeat to his enemies. "The people"—farmers, artisans, shopkeepers, mechanics—had never deserted the Constitution, and when they understood the issues and his position, he believed, they would rally to his support, as they had done in the old days in Tennessee.

This time, however, it was not to be. Johnson's supporters lost hands down, and whatever hopes he had for a presidential coalition party suffered irreparable damage. His opponents managed the sensitive issues very well. Where questions like the tariff and national finances would have embarrassed Republican candidates, the aspirants kept popular attention on southern topics. In addition, they used to good effect the frequency with which Johnson had pardoned southern leaders as well as his reluctance to push the South on controversial issues. Johnson might talk about realigning parties and forming a personal coalition in favor of constitutional government, but to Republicans it looked like an alliance of southern Democrats who wished to destroy the Union and northern Democrats who had refused to help save it.

Perhaps more than any other single issue the plight of the freedmen helped the Republicans. Not that the Republican task was easy; northerners had many qualms about the Negro's role, especially in political matters. Republicans could not campaign for universal Negro suffrage, but they did not have to, for better lines of argument presented themselves. Johnson during 1866 had wanted to hold blacks to the same standards of self-improvement by which white yeomen had succeeded, a view that was logically derived from his general philosophy. Yet mounting evidence in the form of restrictive state legislation and ugly racial clashes showed not only that blacks did not possess the same economic opportunities as prewar whites but that southern landowners hoped to keep freedmen in a permanent state of peonage.

Two serious race riots, one in Memphis in May 1866 and another in New Orleans in July, appalled Republicans. At Memphis a personal altercation led to several days of violence in which the local police and white vigilantes burned and pillaged the black section of town. In New Orleans a dispute over the validity of a constitutional convention supported by black suffragists erupted in police violence that left thirty-seven blacks dead and over a hundred wounded. Johnson claimed that he would have ordered the federal troops at New Orleans to keep the peace had he been informed in time of the true state of affairs, but such episodes fueled arguments that blacks could expect only hostility from southerners and a deaf ear from the President. The Fourteenth Amendment seemed more and more necessary.

Finally, Johnson's personal characteristics lost him support. The campaign degenerated into vituperation on both sides, but Americans found it less objectionable for a newspaper to compare Johnson to Caligula's horse than for the President to take on hecklers in wild tirades. The office of president held a special place, and if its occupant degraded it by his conduct, he could not effectively defend the principles he thought he had followed or the powers he thought the office should have.

Gideon Welles crabbed in November that the campaign had been "mismanaged" in that the President's friends had not resisted Democratic pushiness and had not developed the main constitutional issues. Johnson, keenly disappointed, ignored advice that he recognize his loss of popular favor and allow Congress to legislate on Reconstruction without further hindrance. Not even a nationwide Republican margin of 400,-000 votes weakened his tenacity. False issues misled the people, he believed; in a fair presentation of the truth, the people would bring themselves right.

The lame-duck session of the old Thirty-ninth Congress sat from December to March, its membership unchanged but its determination stiffened. Moderates returned with renewed faith in public acceptance of their efforts, while extremist Republicans hoped for greater influence in the party. Johnson's annual message, a document more restrained than the circumstances might have prompted, offered nothing new; instead, it recapitulated his positions on readmission and the proper workings of the federal system and then turned to other domestic and foreign topics. Horace Greeley thought it "dreary" and about as gripping as one of Franklin Pierce's messages — rather an insult since Johnson had not thought Pierce a very considerable president.

Johnson said nothing about the Fourteenth Amendment directly, though other events made apparent his continuing hostility. During the fall and winter of 1866–67 a number of legislatures took action on the amendment. By New Year's the pattern was clear: five northern states (plus Tennessee) accepted it, and none had yet rejected it, but seven ex-Confederate states turned it down by lopsided counts. Even though the amendment thus encountered no formal opposition (three border states would reject it in the spring) Johnson, whenever asked, advised southern legislatures not to approve it.

While the country considered the amendment, Congress considered more legislation. Some laws aimed at remedying specific conditions in the South. Others sought to solidify the Republican party's position, to strengthen the institutional authority of Congress, and to weaken the office of the presidency. More prominent now than before, legislation of the second type reflected the growing conviction of Republican congressmen that Johnson's opposition to their views of Reconstruction required direct curbs on his power. Indeed, Republican concern over what Johnson had the authority to do, and what he might actually do, even fostered consideration of impeachment during early 1867.

On January 5, the new cycle of vetoes began as Johnson rejected a bill, similar to one the Senate had buried a year before, to extend the suffrage to blacks in the District of Columbia. Since the voters of Washington in December 1865 almost unanimously rejected Negro suffrage, Johnson asserted that the bill clearly violated the concept of popular will and that legislative excesses were just as dangerous as executive ones. Using the *argumentum ad horrendum,* he claimed that Washington Negroes were proportionately more numerous and less well educated than those of the few northern states like Massachusetts that allowed them to vote, and hence "they could readily be made subservient to the purposes of designing persons." An indiscriminate grant of suffrage with only a one-year residence requirement would encourage thousands of blacks from surrounding states to move to Washington, thus making "the white population a subordinate element in the body politic."

Seldom in his presidency could Johnson defend the people against having to accept something they had unmistakably said they did not want, and he made full use of the opportunity. He also stated his belief that the veto was "wholly negative and conservative in its character," a point he had first made in the House during Polk's administration and which complemented his warnings about legislative usurpation. Such arguments carried no weight, however, and Congress overrode the veto.

The most important law of the spring of 1867 was the First Reconstruction Act. This law, a final version of which by the moderate Senator John Sherman triumphed over a harsher draft by the more radical Stevens, firmly placed Reconstruction in the hands of Congress and assigned the on-site administrative role to the United States Army. It divided the South (except Tennessee) into five military districts, each under the command of a presidentially appointed general officer. Although the state governments produced by Johnson's program remained intact, the army received clear powers of supersedure. Generals could allow state and local courts to continue in operation, or they could establish military commissions to try civilians. The army had been physically present in the South since 1865, though its authority had been a subject of considerable confusion until the Reconstruction Act passed.

The new law also established a political process at the conclusion of which the states might, if Congress chose, once again enjoy representation. This process involved registration of voters, election of a convention to draft a new state constitution, revision of franchise laws to include blacks and exclude Confederate leaders, and ratification of the Fourteenth Amendment. No one disqualified from officeholding under the amendment could participate in the electoral process under the act.

Johnson submitted a scathing veto, based extensively on a draft by Jeremiah Sullivan Black, a member of Buchanan's cabinet. The measure was in "palpable" violation of the Constitution most notably because military trials offended the Bill of Rights but for a host of other reasons as well. Far from restoring a republican form of government, it gave the South an "absolute despotism" of military rule: "No master ever had a control so absolute over the slaves as this bill gives to the military officers over both white and colored persons." On these points he now had the backing of the Supreme Court, which, in the 1866 case *Ex parte Milligan,* had ruled martial law unconstitutional in time of peace where civil courts were functioning. Since Johnson viewed the South as being at peace and since civil courts were open even though they often winked at crimes against blacks and loyal whites, he quoted at length from the Court's opinion.

As for the franchise, Johnson asserted that blacks had not asked to vote (he forgot Frederick Douglass' visit a year earlier) and that "the vast majority of them have no idea what it means." The whole thing amounted to "Africanizing" the South in violation of the "universally acknowledged rule of constitutional law," which left the matter to the states. And if votes did not produce prescribed results, "neither blacks nor whites can be relieved from the slavery which the bill imposes upon them."

Here Johnson seemed to forget that his own 1865 program had involved some degree of coercion, for he had always imposed some requirements on state action. He distinguished the cases by distinguishing the motives. "It was to punish the gross crime of defying the Constitution and to vindicate its supreme authority" that the North prosecuted the war and he developed his program of Reconstruction; by comparison, Congress sought "to change the entire structure and character of the State governments and to compel them by force" to adopt prescribed laws against their will. As always, the central question of Reconstruction was the proper exercise of federal power, and Johnson, in spite of constant calls for protection for blacks and Unionists, would not travel beyond the War Aims Resolutions of 1861.

As Johnson observed, the Reconstruction Act highlighted the basic flaw in Congress' constitutional philosophy: by stating in the preamble that no legal governments existed in the South, Congress in effect admitted, after fighting to preserve the Union, that the South had destroyed it by secession. Many people, however, thought this point moot rather than mischievous, and Congress, having the necessary votes, was not disposed to debate niceties of constitutional philosophy with the President. Both houses, by votes of 138 to 51 and 38 to 10, repassed the bill on the same day the veto went in.

Johnson accused Congress of "looking solely to the attainment of political ends" and of failing "to consider the rights it transgresses, the law which it violates, or the institutions which it imperils." This oversimplified analysis of congressional motivation ignored the commitment to aid for blacks, only partially a political element, and concern for the security of the Union, even less a political consideration, which influenced many Republicans. Far from being either uniform or simple, the motives that drove Republicans of differing opinions to cooperate on legislation were complex, and in this contest for power neither the Republicans nor Johnson could claim that virtue was exclusively theirs.

Yet some legislation did have overtly partisan motives, and certain enactments could imperil the institutional balance within the federal government. On January 22 Congress altered its own calendar so that the first session of the new Fortieth Congress, instead of starting in December, would meet on March 4, the day the Thirty-ninth expired. This law, the constitutionality of which Attorney General Stanbery doubted but which Johnson did not bother to veto, had the sole purpose of enabling Congress to be on hand during most of 1867 in case Johnson should take actions that required a legislative check. Also in January the Republicans put up Nebraska and Colorado again, now with the proviso that both states agree never to discriminate against blacks; both bills drew vetoes, but this time the Nebraska measure triumphed, and Johnson dutifully issued the proclamation of statehood on March 1.

Together with the First Reconstruction Act Johnson received two measures that seriously undermined his presidential authority. A rider attached to the Army Appropriations Act attempted to weaken Johnson's role as Commander-in-Chief. Republicans feared that Johnson might issue orders to generals in the South that circumvented congressional intentions. The provision specified that Grant as Commanding General of the army could not be unwillingly assigned to duty outside of Washington; that all orders to the army from the President or

Secretary of War had to go through Grant; and that orders not so routed were void. Drafted by Stanton and radical Congressman George Boutwell, the provision openly affirmed what many already believed: that both Stanton and Grant now agreed more with Congress than with Johnson. Unquestionably unconstitutional, the provision was part of a vital appropriations bill, and so Johnson signed it under protest.

The other March 2 statute regulated the "tenure of certain civil offices." To protect Republican officeholders, the statute required senatorial approval to remove any civil official whose appointmet had required senatorial consent. Cabinet members could hold on throughout "the term of the President by whom they may have been appointed, and for one month thereafter, subject to removal by and with the advice and consent of the Senate." This provision, the meaning of which subsequently caused great difficulty, arose out of a disagreement among proponents of the bill over whether Cabinet members, and particularly Stanton, should be protected. Evidence of misconduct, crime, or incapacity arising during a senatorial recess enabled the president to suspend temporarily an official, subject to concurrence when the Senate reconvened.

The whole Cabinet, especially Stanton, called the act unconstitutional and advised Johnson to veto it. The result was a quiet message, largely Seward's work, that recounted the history of debate on the removal power and stated that the question was "settled ... by construction, settled by precedent, settled by the practice of the Government, and settled by statute": the president, as part of his constitutionally assigned executive authority, exercised the power of removal independently of the Senate. Any other method would weaken his ability to see that the laws were faithfully executed and therefore to carry out his presidential oath. The analysis had historical validity and some philsophical merit, but Congress overrode the veto, 138 to 40 in the House and 35 to 11 in the Senate.

One year to the day after the Tenure of Office Act passed, Johnson would be awaiting trial, having been impeached for allegedly violating its provisions. That drama climaxed an increasingly bitter struggle over power, which reached a watershed with the legislation of the spring of 1867. The new laws set forth the outline of a congressional plan of Reconstruction, identified the agency that would oversee the plan, and laid the groundwork for action should Johnson interfere. His course thus far had been well within his constitutional powers, and while Republicans recoiled at his indecorous speeches and questioned his attitude toward themselves, the blacks, and the South, his official acts had revealed no disposition to travel beyond the law in pursuing his own policy.

Yet Republicans also knew that their legislative course was carrying them ever further from principles that Johnson could approve. A year earlier, in the spring of 1866, some—mistakenly—thought he could have approved the Freedmen's Bureau and Civil Rights measures; but if he could not approve them, and the Fourteenth Amendment, he could hardly have approved the Reconstruction Act. By February 1868 Johnson's efforts to lessen the impact of the congressional program appeared to include a specific violation of law. The congressional response of impeachment represented, instead of another attack on Johnson's policies, an attack on him and on the presidential office even though Republicans viewed it as a necessary defensive move.

Impeachment, however, was no sudden event. Indeed, Congress first considered impeachment while it was also drafting the crucial spring legislation of 1867. Random talk about impeachment dated from the autumn of 1865 when a few editors began spicing up their columns with speculation. In the spring of 1866, after the first vetoes, impeachment talk increased; by the end of the year it figured more prominently in both public and private discussion, but those who supported it were still ultraradicals like Ben Butler, Thaddeus Stevens, and Zachariah Chandler.

Strong considerations worked against impeachment, however. Many Republican moderates believed that Johnson's opposition to congressional plans for Reconstruction had not involved any violation of law or anything else that could properly fall under the heading of "high crimes and misdemeanors." Impeachment based on ill-considered charges would do more harm than good. Business interests also doubted its wisdom and feared that it would harm national credit and financial stability.

Dangers of a party schism notwithstanding, extremists such as Stevens and Boutwell pushed ahead when Congress met in December 1866, and on January 7 resolutions to inquire into grounds for impeachment came up on the floor of the House. An even more extreme resolution, directly impeaching Johnson for high crimes and misdemeanors stemming from alleged corrupt use of his powers to veto, appoint, and pardon, among other things, also demanded attention. This last was the product of Ohio's James M. Ashley, whose bizarre beliefs included the conviction that Zachary Taylor had also been murdered and that Johnson had conspired in Lincoln's assassination. The House, rather than create the select committee the radicals wanted, ordered all such resolutions to the Judiciary Committee, staffed with several moderates.

When the committee began its hearings in February, Ashley and his friends held center stage and went on one fishing expedition after another through Johnson's private financial records, official correspondence, pardon and appointment papers, and affidavits by anyone willing to testify about anything. Nothing was found because nothing was there to be found. A man with some significant weaknesses, both personal and political, Johnson was nevertheless hardly the suborner of murder, the corrupt dispenser of favors, or the deliberate inciter of southern racial violence that Ashley and others conjured up. The committee drew no conclusions but recommended that the Fortieth Congress continue the investigation. Legislators had at least put Johnson on notice that his conduct bore watching even if the forum was very like a circus ring.

The President viewed these proceedings with remarkable equanimity. He did not lash out at Congress in wild tirades; Washington's birthday passed quietly this year. The aspersions on his character stung him more than the political accusations, and sometime in March his private secretary entered a presidential comment in his notebook: "I have had a son killed, a son-in-law die during the last battle at Nashville, another son has thrown himself away, a second son-in-law is in no better condition. I think I have had sorrow enough without having my bank account examined by a Committee of Congress." In an extended interview on March 5 Johnson observed, "For the slights and indignities, the unconstitutional curtailments and dishonors which the recent Congress has attempted to cast upon me for my unflinching and unalterable devotion to my constitutional oath, and to the best interests of the whole country, according to my best judgment and experience, I am only sorry as regards the indignities sought to be imposed on my high office, but unmoved as regards myself." Certain that "the day of wiser thought and sounder estimate" would soon arrive, Johnson added that he expected his own "vindication" by "the justice of that future" he saw approaching.

Not merely approaching, but arriving, that very day was the first session of the Fortieth Congress, which met briefly in March and again in July and November—and it offered Johnson no vindication. The March meeting produced a Second Reconstruction Act, made necessary because the first one lacked procedural details. The new law obliged prospective voters to swear that they were not disfranchised for participation in the rebellion, and final judgment on eligibility lay with the registrars, who were military appointees and sometimes military officers.

In his brief veto Johnson argued that any convention chosen with such military supervision could hardly represent the people and could only produce a constitution "arbitrarily dictated by Congress and formed under the restraint of military rule." He added, "If ever the American citizen should be left to the free exercise of his own judgment it is when he is engaged in the work of forming the fundamental law under which he is to live." Johnson also returned, with greater force than in recent months, to the subject of Negro suffrage. He noted that Congress considered existing southern constitutions not to be "loyal and republican," and by Congress' own requirements, the only thing needed to make them "loyal and republican" was Negro suffrage. By that standard, "the work of reconstruction may as well begin in Ohio as in Virginia, in Pennsylvania as in North Carolina." The override seemed almost automatic.

Also in March the House Judiciary Committee got fresh authorization from the new Congress to continue its labors. This the committee did for the rest of the spring, but in spite of a parade of witnesses in high places and low, and Ashley's unbridled efforts, no impeachable conduct came to light. On June 3 the committee adjourned, standing 5 to 4 against impeachment. Even the vote and the adjournment gave Johnson no comfort, for the committee also determined that the President, though constitutionally unimpeachable, deserved public opprobrium, and by a party vote of 7 to 2 it passed a resolution of censure. Well might Johnson have reflected back almost forty years to Andrew Jackson's time, when Old Hickory's bank politics earned him a resolution of censure from the Senate, since the House would not impeach him. Had the President been in a musing mood, he might have reflected how, as a freshman Tennessee legislator, he had helped to table a resolution instructing the Tennessee senators to vote to "expunge" the censure from the Senate's journal.

Johnson, however, was not in a musing mood. He did at times, though with diminishing frequency, turn to lighter things, and there are accounts of his reciting poetry and other literature from memory to his secretary, Colonel Moore. The colonel, in January 1867, noted Johnson's "very high conception of language" and how he favored pieces like Byron's poems on Waterloo and Thomas Gray's *Elegy Written in a Country Churchyard.* From the latter Johnson repeated several times the lines "Full many a gem of purest ray serene / The dark unfathomed caves of ocean bear" and remarked that they possessed "both grandeur and solemnity." Johnson's pleasure in such literary pictures at such a time was indicative, for his political career was certainly embarked upon stormy seas.

Yet if Johnson was no longer in control of Reconstruction policy, he was certainly in control of his own responses to Congress and of his efforts to maintain as much influence as possible. He did not pursue a rash, headlong policy of blind opposition, and though he often said that he did not fear impeachment, he stuck to his intention of keeping his opposition within constitutional bounds. He also agreed that the Attorney General should resist an April effort by Mississippi to get a Supreme Court injunction against his execution of the Reconstruction Act on the ground that the President, as a representative of the people, could not be sued.

Since the First Reconstruction Act made it Johnson's duty to appoint the district commanders, he appointed them and accepted the list proposed by Grant. The spread of views was interesting. Phillip Sheridan, headquartered at New Orleans, was fully in sympathy with Republican radicals; Daniel Sickles at Charleston and John Pope at Atlanta came very close behind. John Schofield at Richmond held moderate conservative opinions, and Edward O. C. Ord at Vicksburg fell somewhere in the middle.

All except Pope had at least some prior experience in the South, and while Johnson could hardly have liked the choice of Sheridan and Sickles, nothing would be gained by needlessly antagonizing Grant. The victor of Appomattox was clearly the most popular man in the country. His opinions on Reconstruction now had a strong Republican flavor, but Johnson still had cordial official relations with him. Such was not the case with Stanton, and had not been for months. Gideon Welles often noted Stanton's duplicity in his diary, and Johnson shared the opinion. In April 1867 Colonel Moore recorded Johnson's belief that Stanton's collusion with congressional radicals had undercut the chances for an early solution to Reconstruction along Johnsonian lines.

Johnson's deteriorating relations with Stanton made the

maintenance of official harmony with Grant that much more important. Some considerations were political. Grant was the obvious front runner for the Republican presidential nomination in 1868, and Johnson derived a political advantage of his own from keeping Grant close to the administration. Wartime events had made Grant and Butler enemies, and since Butler was a front-rank impeacher, Grant might serve as a valuable counterweight.

Beyond political considerations, however, relations between President and Commanding General had a very important institutional dimension. The army, made a part of the executive branch by the Constitution, served as the enforcement agency for a legislative program of Reconstruction. There was nothing troublesome about that, at least in theory, because the army was doing its recognized duty when called upon to enforce national law. The difficulty arose when Congress, to blunt Johnson's opposition, trenched upon the constitutional prerogatives of the President with its stipulations of March 2 ragarding the command of the army. The effect was to give two subordinates a legislatively sanctioned position as blocks to the orders of their constitutional superior.

The case of Stanton had all the political difficulties inherent when a troublesome Cabinet member refused to step down, with the added complications of the Tenure of Office Act. The case of Grant appeared at first to be simpler, at least in view of the professional soldier's lifelong education to obey superior orders. But what if there came a point when constitutional obligations to the Commander-in-Chief clashed with professional loyalty to the army? For the latter impulse was very strong in Grant, and the army's delicate duties in Secessia, for which many officers lacked adequate preparation, often led to requests for guidance from the Commanding General. Grant sought to make sure that generals had enough authority to perform their duties effectively while at the same time shielding the army from embarrassment.

Two specific issues gave trouble during the spring and summer of 1867. One was the definition of criteria for disfranchisement, and the authority of registering boards; the other was the military power to remove civil officials. In March and April, Schofield and Sheridan both requested an interpretation of the disfranchisement sections by the Attorney General. Johnson directed Stanbery to prepare it, and all the Cabinet except Stanton approved it. The complete draft, dated May 24, interpreted the law narrowly on the question of what conduct worked disfranchisement, and also denied the power of registrars to determine eligibility. Johnson had the opinion sent to the five district commanders "for their information" and to ensure uniformity in administration of the law; an accompanying letter of transmittal from the Assistant Adjutant General bore the closing statement, "By order of the President." Sheridan asked Grant if Stanbery's opinion was an "order"; Grant replied that it had not been distributed in proper form and added, "Nor can I suppose that the President intended it to have such force."

Grant had not checked with Johnson, and the episode marked the first time he had used subterfuge to circumvent the President's wishes. Grant believed that Stanbery's opinion made it impossible to keep rebels out of the political process and that a separate opinion restricting the generals' power to remove civil officials made it impossible to deal with those who interfered with military actions. When Johnson realized what Grant had done, he did not make an issue of it but chose to regard the generals' possession of Stanbery's opinion as sufficient.

Congress promptly overruled the Attorney General. During a brief session in July it passed by strict party vote the Third Reconstruction Act. Drafted by Stanton and Grant, it confirmed the generals' power to remove officials and control all aspects of registration of voters; broadly defined conduct warranting disfranchisement; and allowed Grant to remove officials on his own initiative. The district commanders and their appointees could ignore "any opinion of any civil officer of the United States" and should construe "liberally" all Reconstruction measures "to the end that all the intents thereof may be fully and perfectly carried out." Johnson's veto message began by reciting anew all of the dangers of military despotism, a response evoked by the assignment to the army of more direct control over civil and political affairs than ever before. The President also emphasized the weaknesses, both theoretically and in practice between 1861 and 1867, of Congress' position on the constitutional status of the southern states.

These things he had said before. The last three paragraphs, however, made points of much greater significance, for Johnson now restated the principal current theme of his struggle with Congress: "Within a period of less than a year the legislation of Congress has attempted to strip the executive department of the Government of some of its essential powers." He noted that the Constitution required him to see that the laws were faithfully executed and therefore "gives him the choice of the agents, and makes them subject to his control and supervision." Johnson recognized that Congress had attempted to make the agents independent of him, and thus "any attempt on the part of the President to assert his own constitutional power may, under pretense of law, be met by official insubordination. It is to be feared that these military officers, looking to the authority given by these laws rather than to the letter of the Constitution, will recognize no authority but the commander of the district and the General of the Army."

Control of the agents meant control over federal actions in the South. So it had always been. Yet mid-1867 marked a turning point. In 1865 Johnson, acting alone, could focus upon a simple policy leading to quick restoration of a South in which state recognition of the failure of secession and war accompanied national recognition of local control of traditionally local issues. The legislation of 1866, while still directed toward events in the South, led to the institutional conflict between presidency and Congress over federal functions and power, a dimension that Johnson clearly realized at the time. By the summer of 1867 the course of legislation had so far removed the reins from Johnson's hands—and by direct encroachment on presidential functions—that institutional aspects assumed high priority. Johnson still wished to control affairs in the South, but defense of the presidency had greater importance, both immediate and long-range.

It was hardly surprising that after raising in his veto the issue of presidential prerogative, Johnson said: "If there were no other objection than this to this proposed legislation, it would be sufficient. Whilst I hold the chief executive authority of the United States, whilst the obligation rests upon me to see that all the laws are faithfully executed, I can never willingly surrender that trust or the powers given for its execution." His devotion to Jackson's philosophy, his longing while in Congress to see strong executives, his own frustrations as prewar governor, and his experiences as Lincoln's designee in Tennessee gave him the desire to be a strong president and brought him to the defense of the office when he saw it being attacked. The contours of Johnson's character etched more deeply the straight lines of his principles and the profile of his life's service. Often criticized for rigid adherence to abstract notions, Johnson never turned away from a dispute over them and made personal crusades of the ones he believed he embodied. Indeed, the issues and course of Reconstruction followed closely the pattern most likely to rouse the legacies of Johnson's personal history.

Since any coalition of Democrats and conservative or moderate Republicans, whatever its early chances might have been, was now clearly impossible, Johnson's only avenue for personal ambition was the Democratic presidential nomination in 1868. He hoped to have it; but if the presidency itself were destroyed, it would be an empty honor. And he certainly believed that the presidency was in danger. When he said, as he often did with one expletive or another, that he cared nothing about impeachment, he meant it in a personal sense, not an institutional one. He had been maligned so often for positions he believed to be right that personal attacks were nothing new, but he did not want to be responsible for a serious weakening of the presidential office. The general pattern of Johnson's decisions during 1867 reflected a cautious desire to exert as much influence over Reconstruction as possible and to preserve presidential prerogatives without giving Congress an opportunity, through impeachment, to attack the presidency directly.

There were two ironies in this situation. The man who sought to be a strong president now in fact occupied a position of weakness in which he could not control constitutional subordinates and from which, according to his critics, he had brought disgrace upon the office itself. Furthermore, the man who often talked about his presidential oath to see that the laws were faithfully executed was in fact no longer trusted by Congress, or by some of his subordinates, to carry out that duty. These two ironies stood clearly revealed in events following the Third Reconstruction Act.

By the end of July, Johnson decided that he would oust Sheridan from the New Orleans post and Stanton from the War Department. Sheridan's course, marked by the removal of the governors of Louisiana and Texas as well as lesser officials, had been entirely too extreme for Johnson. Stanton had simply become unacceptable as a presidential adviser. The President had long held Stanton responsible for withholding a telegram asking for instructions at the outbreak of the New Orleans riot of 1866, and more recently he blamed Stanton, whose War Department ran the trial of the Lincoln assassins, for not ensuring that he knew about a recommendation by the military commission for clemency for Mrs. Mary Surratt. The President had on several occasions been displeased with Stanton's unwillingness in the Cabinet to take a position or to give a direct response when asked for an opinion, and he knew that Stanton was a conduit by which information about Cabinet discussions reached the secretary's congressional intimates.

Friends and advisers urged Johnson for months to get rid of Stanton, and his waiting till the thirteenth hour perplexed many people. At least, they thought, he should have moved while the Tenure bill was still in Congress. Johnson, however, occupied a difficult position. Stanton was popular, and since he had ignored repeated hints that his resignation would be welcome—especially after he remarked during discussion of the Tenure bill that no honorable man would stay on in the face of a desired resignation—the matter presented delicate problems. Johnson waited, in the hope that something would encourage Stanton to quit. Tired and in ill health, Stanton would have preferred to leave the government and return to private law practice, but his strong beliefs about Reconstruction and Johnson's threat to congressional policies kept him on.

Finally, the President decided that waiting any longer would avail nothing. On August 1 he asked Grant whether he would take over the War Department on a temporary basis; Grant opposed relieving Stanton but said he would perform any "public duty" required of him and then wrote Johnson a letter denying the President's power to tamper with Stanton in view of the Tenure of Office Act. Johnson and Welles discussed this letter on August 3, and when Welles remarked that Grant was "going over" to the radicals, Johnson replied, "I am aware of it. I have no doubt that most of these offensive measures have emanated from the War Department." Johnson perceived Stanton as having turned Grant against the administration, and Grant as being so malleable that if gotten away from Stanton's influence and brought into the Cabinet, he could be corrected. This analysis, however, assigned too large a role to conspiracy and too small a role to principle. Nor did Grant prove to be as malleable as Johnson wished.

On August 5 a presidential note solicited Stanton's resignation. He refused. After a few days' hiatus, during which Johnson considered Frank Blair and General James B. Steedman as replacements—the former a major Democratic figure and the latter a lesser light but a Democrat of long presidential friendship—Johnson returned to his earlier choice of Grant. On Sunday morning, August 11, Johnson and Grant met once more and had a friendly exchange of views. To the President's inquiry whether there was anything personal between them, Grant responded negatively, but added that he had thought Johnson ought not to have objected to the Fourteenth Amendment. He neglected to add that in private correspondence he had scoffed at recent vetoes as being "riduculous." Johnson reiterated that Stanton must go; Grant made no further protest and agreed to take the position.

The official correspondence went out the next day, and the choice of words was deliberate. Johnson "suspended" Stanton and appointed Grant as "Secretary of War *ad interim*" under executive authority granted by the "Consititution and laws of the United States." Though he did not refer specifically to the Tenure of Office Act, Johnson had in fact followed the procedure therein provided for dispensing with an official during a recess of the Senate. He could therefore not be accused of violating the law, and by citing a general source of authority, he could maintain his view of executive power in the face of a law he believed unconstitutional. Stanton blustered but departed, and whatever else might happen, Johnson could at least look forward to several months without the peppery Ohioan. The suspicious Welles even thought Grant rather liked the new order of things.

Whatever Grant liked, he certainly disliked some events that followed in quick succession. The Sheridan case, sidetracked when Johnson decided that Stanton should be the main target, now awaited resolution. Except for Welles, the Cabinet had qualms about removing him because of his popularity, but no law protected him, and on August 17 Johnson drafted an order replacing him with George Thomas. This order he sent to Grant for comment; Grant protested, but the order went out on August 19. To preserve as much of Sheridan's work as possible, Grant ordered Thomas to continue in force whatever orders existed in the Fifth District when he arrived. Thomas, however, pleaded ill health and recommended Winfield Scott Hancock, a strong Democrat whom Johnson preferred anyway. After several days of sparring between Johnson and Grant, during which time the general wrote and subsequently withdrew a statement that Johnson regarded as an "insubordinate" political essay, Hancock's transfer from Kansas to New Orleans took effect, though he did not actually reach there until late November. Sickles, too, found himself removed from the Charleston command, his most recent offense having been an interference with the operation of federal courts.

Not only were Stanton, Sheridan, and Sickles out, but, it seemed, the rebels were back in—or at least as far back in as another proclamation of pardon could bring them. Johnson asserted in a proclamation of September 7, drafted largely by Seward, that because southern conditions were favorable, and because a "retaliatory or vindictive policy, attended by unnecessary disqualifications, pains, penalties, confiscations, and disfranchisements" did more harm than good, the benefits of his May 1865 proclamation should now apply to most of those previously excluded. He thus offered, in exchange for an oath of future loyalty, to all who "directly or indirectly, participated in the late rebellion," a pardon and "restoration of all privileges, immunities, and rights of property" except slaves. The only exceptions were the Confederate President, Vice-President, Cabinet, diplomatic officers, governors, and flag officers of the army and navy, in addition to the Lincoln assassins and persons who had mistreated prisoners of war. The restoration clause of this proclamation was broader than the 1865 measure, for Johnson wished to remove as many obstacles as possible to full participation by southerners.

The removals and the proclamation added more fuel to the impeachers' fires, and even moderate Republicans began to observe that impeachment awaited only a plausible excuse. Johnson seemed unperturbed and even showed more joviality in September than in the preceding three months. On September 17 he rode out to Antietam with what Welles called "a pleasant miscellaneous company" to celebrate the fifth anniversary of the battle. Johnson's party left the field after the regular program concluded, but several Republican governors stayed on for impromptu speeches, thus delaying the train, and so Welles did not get home until nearly two in the morning.

More irritating to Welles than the loss of sleep was the thought of radical politicians campaigning in a "national graveyard," but the autumn always brought local elections, and even though there were fewer contests than in 1866, all ears harkened for the sound of rustling ballots, Johnson's especially. Back in July he had closed his veto of the Third Reconstruction Act with reference to the ballot as a remedy for legislative excesses and said, "I am still hopeful of the future, and that in the end the rod of despotism will be broken, and the armed heel of power lifted from the necks of the people, and the principles of a violated Constitution preserved." Futures, of course, weave portents and shadows into uncertain tapestries. But one element of the future seemed clear, from the perspective of a sprinkly September day, while clickety-clacking along on the Baltimore and Ohio. Congress could not act upon impeachment until after the people had another say at the polls in November.

X

"Damn Them!"

1868–1869

FOR MOST of November 1867 Gideon Welles lay sick in his bed. He lacked energy even to pursue his favorite pastime of filling his diary volumes with fact and rumor, speculation and canard, offhand comment and labored analysis about politics and personalities. Visitors cheered him, and he later noted with quiet appreciation that the President had sometimes dropped in twice a day. It was typical of Johnson to be so solicitous of the health of a friend, and Welles was the firmest presidential supporter in a Cabinet that, save for Grant, accepted Johnson's views on Reconstruction. Indeed, Welles was even more extreme than Johnson himself on some points and freely expressed his opinions. He recognized limitations in Johnson's personal style — less often ones in his own viewpoint — and Johnson clearly thought his Navy Secretary a valued cohort.

Among the subjects of bedside chats was the autumn elections. The tide seemed to be turning. From September through November the Democrats registered successes in California, Ohio, Pennsylvania, Maryland, New Jersey, and New

York. The season posted its biggest pleasures for Johnson in the defeat of black suffrage measures in Kansas, Ohio, and Minnesota. Although some contests highlighted local issues like prohibition and financial questions, when Democrats attacked radical Reconstruction they made inroads upon the Republicans, and black suffrage offered special opportunities.

Johnson's annual message exploited these weaknesses. Harsher than any previous message, it lectured the Congress on constitutional philosophy and then launched into a more severe denunciation of black suffrage than Johnson had ever made in an official paper. Asserting that the whole purpose of congressional Reconstruction was to enfranchise blacks and disfranchise whites in sufficient numbers to give the blacks a political majority, he lamented "the process of clothing the negro race with the political privileges torn from white men." There could be no doubt about his opinion of comparative abilities: "It is the glory of white men to know that they have had these qualities in sufficient measure to build upon this continent a great political fabric and to preserve its stability for more than ninety years, while in every other part of the world all similar experiments have failed. But . . . it must be acknowledged that in the progress of nations negroes have shown less capacity for government than any other race of people. No independent government of any form has ever been successful in their hands. On the contrary, wherever they have been left to their own devices they have shown a constant tendency to relapse into barbarism."

Johnson also explored the constitutional avenues open to a president who perceived himself a savior of the people from the dangers of unconstitutional laws. Forceful resistance he ruled out as leading to civil war. "A faithful and conscientious magistrate will concede very much to honest error, and something even to perverse malice, before he will endanger the public peace; and he will not adopt forcible measures, or such as might lead to force, as long as those which are peaceable remain open to him or to his constituents."

The course remaining open to his constituents was the ballot, well used of late. The course remaining open to him personally he did not fully explain, but "judicial remedy" clearly played a part. He observed that "some open tribunal, independent of party politics" would be a more appropriate place than the Senate to test the validity of executive removals. In language at once theoretical and particular, at once vague and directed, the President eschewed rash actions but warned that he had not yet exhausted his efforts to assuage what he considered to be the harmful effects of congressional Reconstruction and that he was moving closer to a court test of his constitutional powers.

Other tests of other constitutional powers were in the making, however. The House Judiciary Committee had met again in November, and now, because one New York congressman changed his mind over the Stanton and Sheridan cases, favored impeachment by a margin of 5 to 4. When Johnson heard, he just said, "If it is so, so let it be." The committee offered a catalogue of culpability including the issues of pardon, appointment, fomenting violence in the South, restoration of rebel property, and even the vetoes, but on December 7 the floor vote came: 57 for impeachment, 108 against. Over sixty of the nays were Republicans.

The test revealed a party with serious problems. Republicans could not agree on the conduct of the incumbent, nor had they restored the Union themselves. Johnson opposed Congress in action after action and had not yet stepped over the line. What more could he do short of some violent onset against Congress—the imminence of which the brisk winds of rumor constantly circulated. Indeed, advice along that very line often came from mad scribblers with a few postage stamps to spare, or more precisely, to waste, since Johnson could hardly have contemplated such a thing. But he resolved to continue to act in appropriate spheres.

The opportunity soon arose. General Hancock's first order in New Orleans extolled the virtues of civil supremacy over military power. Johnson thought it deserved the official thanks of Congress. Congress laughed. Two weeks later, however, the laughter stopped when Johnson, at the request of southern conservatives, removed General Pope from the Atlanta command. Among other objectionable actions Pope had adopted electoral districts for the Georgia constitutional convention that gave blacks, a minority of the registered voters, control of a majority of the seats. Johnson also removed General Ord from the Arkansas-Mississippi district, but he acted at Ord's own request countersigned by Grant.

These events were sideshows, however. If unhorsing the dashing and highly popular cavalryman Sheridan did not cause impeachment, silencing the bombastic Pope, equally radical now but a wartime loser, would hardly bring it about. Besides, the Stanton case, now in a formal phase, again occupied center stage. On December 12, a presidential message laid the suspension before the Senate. Johnson had at first intended only to send a brief message, but Stanbery talked him into sending a more elaborate one, and the result was a masterpiece.

The message dealt equally skillfully with the personal and constitutional sides of the question. In April 1865 Stanton had supported presidential authority to form a Reconstruction program; two years later he no longer supported a presidential course that had grown out of that program, and a mutual lack of confidence had gradually developed. The only episode treated at length was the famous case of the tardy telegram: General Absalom Baird, temporarily in command in New Orleans in August 1866, had wired to Stanton for instructions two days before the bloody riot, and Stanton had neither answered nor shown the telegram to Johnson. Because the President, ever since, had been unfairly blamed for the violence, he took the opportunity to set the record straight; in fact, it did open a few congressional eyes. The message, without any harsh or improper language, painted Stanton as an unfaithful, untrustworthy, and personally objectionable agent who had boxed himself into a corner and now looked foolish. He had advised Johnson emphatically in March 1867 that the Tenure of Office Act was unconstitutional, and now that it was passed, cited it in August in his own defense.

Upon his suspension in August, Stanton denied Johnson's right "under the Constitution and laws of the United States" to do so. The presidential message handled that part of the record carefully. The Constitution made the president responsible for the executive branch and prescribed an oath of office; surely those great principles allowed him to divest himself of such as Stanton. The law establishing the War Department in 1789 gave the president "the unlimited right to remove the head of the Department." And the message deftly skirted the Tenure of Office Act, whose vague wording had even earlier raised doubts whether Stanton came within its purview. Since Johnson thought the law unconstitutional, he had never specifically cited it in his August suspension order; nor did he now cite it as the source of any authority; nor did he even say his message was made in compliance with it; nor, for that matter, did he even submit his message "for the action of the Senate." He merely submitted it. Yet in fact the August suspension, the *ad interim* appointment, and the December message followed precisely the procedures in the Tenure Act. Having once said the law was unconstitutional, Johnson officially ignored it, found necessary sources of authority elsewhere, yet protected himself against charges of having violated it. Grant was still in, Stanton was still out, Johnson was still in the clear, and the Senate could make its own way out of the quandary.

For a month the Senate considered the case, and on January 13, by a vote of 35 to 6, the chamber refused to concur in Stanton's suspension. Grant, even more than Johnson, now held the spotlight. Would he yield the office, or would he resist? Johnson and Grant discussed the matter on at least two occasions in the two weeks before the Senate acted. On both occasions the undecided general said he would at least surrender the office back to the President in time for Johnson to appoint someone else. The second meeting occurred on Saturday, January 11, and Johnson clearly believed he then received Grant's promise to resign early if he preferred not to resist the Senate's expected action. However, on the morning of January 14, Grant locked the War Department office, gave the key to Assistant Adjutant General E. D. Townsend, sent a note of resignation to Johnson, and went back to his headquarters as Commanding General. Stanton picked up the key and walked back in.

According to private secretary Moore, "The President was indignant at what he considered Grant's duplicity." Johnson immediately summoned Grant to a Cabinet meeting and with what Welles called a "cold" manner but without "anything approaching incivility" asked the "abject" general to explain. Grant hummed and hawed, said he had been busy with a number of "little things," and besides, he had only recently realized that the Tenure of Office Act provided jail and a fine for continuing to hold an office in defiance of senatorial non-concurrence.

Next morning the Washington *Intelligencer,* an administration organ, described the Cabinet session and upbraided Grant, who immediately rounded up Sherman and visited Johnson to complain. Sherman later recalled that as they left, Grant turned and suggested that Johnson issue an order "that we of the army are not bound to obey the orders of Mr. Stanton as Secretary of War." The motive for this suggestion was not clear, and Johnson did not immediately comply. When after repeated requests he did so, Grant responded that because Johnson had not, after January 14, countermanded Stanton's authority to issue orders to the army, he would assume all of Stanton's orders that purported to have Johnson's approval in fact did.

By now Johnson and Grant had become embroiled in an escalating written controversy, which began with the first *Intelligencer* article and continued into mid-February. Each letter immediately became public, and Johnson also solicited accounts of the January 14 Cabinet meeting from the five members present. On February 3 Grant described "this whole matter, from the beginning to the end, as an attempt to involve me in the resistance of law, for which you hesitated to assume the responsibility in orders, and thus to destroy my character before the country." For no other reason, he thought, would his "honor as a soldier and integrity as a man have been so violently assailed."

Grant's analysis had only partial merit. Even before the Senate acted on January 13, Johnson came to doubt how far he could rely on Grant. If the general would not cooperate further, these was no point in keeping him in the Cabinet, especially since each passing day brought Grant nearer the Republican nomination. While Johnson did not originally seek a violent personal rupture, his possible surprise and certain annoyance at Grant's actions of January 11–14, together with Grant's awkward and indecisive conduct in that same period, offered the President an opportunity to paint the General as a devious and unfaithful subordinate. Of course the newspaper controversy inured to Grant's benefit, since he easily won in a contest of veracity and honor with Johnson. Whether pursuing it was a blunder depends on the viewpoint: the Democrats might appreciate presidential boldness at Grant's expense; the Republicans would surely tote up another debit on Johnson's lengthening ledger.

Grant having stepped aside, his replacement had to be someone willing to evict Stanton if necessary and also to accept a court test. The judicial route had taken on paramount importance in Johnson's mind. Grant's phrase "resistance to law" carried a negative connotation; Johnson would have said "constitutional resistance to unconstitutional law," a phrase suggesting not merely a positive connotation but a manifest duty. He knew full well that the struggle over southern policy had now become an institutional struggle threatening presidential prerogatives. He knew from his mail that conservatives North and South regarded him as the last bulwark against legislative tyranny. He knew that the Supreme Court, too, was a subject of congressional ire, for various measures to curb it were now afoot; when one that restricted its appellate jurisdiction in appeals from military commissions emerged as law in March, he gave it an unsuccessful veto. Such circumstances confirmed Johnson's determination to defend presidential power, and he had already raised in his annual message the propriety of doing so through a judicial test.

For a month Johnson cast about for Stanton's replacement while Stanton hung grimly on, shuffling papers day to day with neither written nor verbal communication across the little street to the White House. The President tried more than once to attract Lieutenant General Sherman with preliminary moves, including a special territorial command at Washington and the brevet rank of General. Sherman had the personal qualities and Reconstruction philosophy Johnson wanted. Besides, Stanton had treated him shabbily when he made well-intentioned political errors in the course of accepting the surrender of Joe Johnston's rebel army after Appomattox. But Sherman's decisiveness also carried him in unsuitable directions, for he hated politics—had, ever since he graduated from West Point the year of the "log cabin and hard cider" foolishness—and cherished Grant—had, ever since their days together before Vicksburg. "Therefore, with my consent, Washington never," he insisted.

Since Sherman refused to oppose Stanton and Grant, Johnson sounded out John Potts, chief clerk of the War Department—not for valorous inclinations, because the man was both afraid of Stanton and beholden to him, but because vacancies left him as the official custodian of records. When Moore broached the idea, Potts quailed and shrank behind his sheaves of accounts and requisitions.

Johnson's ultimate choice proved little better. On February 11 Welles and Johnson discussed the position of Adjutant General, the chief administrative post in the army. For five years Stanton had kept General Lorenzo Thomas, who held the title, out of Washington on make-work assignments (currently touring national cemeteries) and the Assistant Adjutant General ran the office. Not much suffered in the arrangement because Thomas, a sixtyish epitome of the weaknesses of a military system that had never mandated rotation from staff duty to line command, had long since lost his effectiveness.

The point was that Johnson regarded Thomas as "right-minded" and, in view of the importance now attached to the channels whereby orders went to the army, brought the silver-haired gentleman back to his assigned position.

A week later, on February 19, Johnson and Moore discussed Thomas as a potential *ad interim* secretary of war. Moore thought Johnson should wait because Thomas was such a lightweight, but as he recorded Johnson's response: "He said he was determined to remove Stanton. Self respect demanded it and if the people did not respect their Chief Magistrate, enough to sustain him in such a measure, the President ought to resign." On the morning of Friday the twenty-first Johnson signed the fateful letters. Citing his authority under the "Constitution and laws," he now "removed" Stanton and appointed Thomas as Secretary *ad interim.* He also informed the Senate, and later that day he informed the Cabinet almost casually— "[a]fter disposing of regular Cabinet business as we were about rising," noted Welles. "He had, he said, perhaps delayed the step too long. At all events, it was time the issue was settled."

The word *settled* proved to be a trifle inapt. Thomas went to the War Office and sought possession; Stanton stalled for time and asked to gather up his things. Thomas, glowing, genial, and credulous, said he would come back the next day. Meanwhile, in the House, John Covode introduced a resolution impeaching Johnson for high crimes and misdemeanors, and the chamber referred it to the Reconstruction Committee. The Senate decided by a vote of 28 to 6, with twenty abstentions, that Johnson had no constitutional power to remove Stanton, thus prejudging an issue upon which they would subsequently have to try the President.

Preparations for Friday night offered the contrast of fevered caucus and smug revelry. Several of Stanton's congressional friends rushed to the War Department, where they agreed to sleep on couches and help defend the embattled precincts. Thomas went off to a masquerade ball at Willard's Hotel where, a bit too liquored, and stirred to the quick upon hearing from a fellow native-stater that "The eyes of all Delaware are upon you!" he bragged that he would evict Stanton on the morrow, and with force, too, if the ousted secretary dared resist. Next morning, however, the door knocked upon was Thomas's, whither District of Columbia Judge David Cartter, at Stanton's request, had sent a marshal to arrest Thomas for violation of the Tenure Act. Shortly released on bail, Thomas went to the War Department and confronted Stanton. After an altercation that moved from room to room of the suite, Stanton gained the advantage with a bottle, an arm around the general's shoulders, some stroking of the general's hair, and a promise not to have him arrested before breakfast next time.

Johnson, dismayed at Thomas' weakness, at least welcomed the arrest because the case would serve to test the Tenure of Office Act's constitutionality. Stanton, however, shortly dropped the charges, and it became clear that all tests would occur in other forums. On Monday, February 24, the House impeached Johnson; 128 Republicans overwhelmed 47 Democrats. Moore had dinner with the President that day and stayed until news of the vote arrived, at six or thereabouts. "The President took the matter very coolly and was not at all excited," Moore observed. "He simply remarked he thought many of them who voted for it felt more uneasy over the position in which they had put themselves than he did in the position in which they had put him."

Johnson's comment had merit at the time and even more as the spring of 1868 progressed. A number of influential Republicans supported impeachment only because they could see no other way to ensure congressional control of Reconstruction. These had voted against impeachment until the removal of Stanton in apparent violation of law seemed to give a more sinister intensity to the President's course. Moreover, while the strict party vote suggested long-awaited Republican unity, the nature of impeachment itself and the issues relevant in this specific case would soon reveal during the trial several seams along which the coalition might be made to fracture.

Johnson's position still involved the same immediate practical and long-term philosophical elements. Direction of affairs in the South raised the same questions from 1865 about the uses of federal power. Furthermore, Johnson saw impeachment as another episode in a constitutional battle he had waged for years, before there was any need for a Reconstruction policy, before there was a rebellion. He had no doubts, in February 1868, about his role as an exponent of a consistent political philosophy. On February 22 Moore recorded Johnson's view that "if he cannot be President in fact, he will not be President in name alone." A week later: "The President very earnestly said: 'Impeachment of me for violating the Constitution! Damn them! Have I not been struggling ever since I have been in this chair to uphold the Constitution which they trample under foot?'"

Conscious of how his current stand derived from his own life history, Johnson also identified historical characters who seemed to him to fit the same mold. One Sunday after church he reflected upon Addison's *Cato* and analyzed the old Roman for Moore. "Cato was a man, he said, who would not compromise with wrong but being right, died before he would yield. Caesar the Great offered him conditions if he would submit but proud old Cato folded his arms and dictated in hidden terms to Caesar." The circumstances did not completely match, but that was not always a concern when statesmen borrowed images across the span of twenty centuries.

There would soon be ample opportunity to quote the classics at length, for the trial of a president before the Senate on charges brought by the House offered a spectacle for oratorical triumph. It also offered a series of perplexing legal problems. First was the matter, accomplished somewhat out of proper order, of drafting specific articles of impeachment. As finally developed, and approved on March 2–3, eleven articles detailed an assortment of charges.

The first nine articles all involved the events of February 21–22 and alleged violations of the Constitution, federal law, and the presidential oath. Article I charged that the removal of Stanton violated the Tenure of Office Act; Articles II and

III charged another violation in the appointment of Thomas. Articles IV through VII alleged a conspiracy among Johnson, Thomas, and others unnamed to violate the Tenure Act, sieze War Department property, and intimidate Stanton; two of these articles alleged violation of the Conspiracies Act of 1861. Article VIII asserted that Thomas' appointment was for the purpose of unlawfully controlling the disbursement of government funds, and Article IX accused the President of trying to induce General William H. Emory, commanding the Military District of Washington, to violate the law by ignoring Grant and taking orders directly from the White House.

The other two articles got added on the House floor on March 3. Article X, by Butler, was a scissors and paste montage of Johnson's wild speeches during the 1866 swing around the circle, designed to show that the President had been so "unmindful of the high duties of his office and the dignity and proprieties thereof" that he had brought it "into contempt, ridicule, and disgrace, to the great scandal of all good citizens." To this Johnson observed, "I think he has never grasped one of them [the speeches], but I am much obliged to him for again bringing them to public notice. There is really even more truth in them than I supposed they contained." The eleventh article, a Stevens revision of a Wilson draft, was a catchall designed to offer something for everyone. It asserted that in August 1866 Johnson had called Congress a body without constitutional authority to exercise legislative power (since the South was unrepresented) and that hence its enactments were not binding. In pursuance of this statement Johnson's actions of February 21 supposedly showed an intent to defeat the execution of the Tenure of Office Act, the Command of the Army rider, and the Reconstruction Act.

The articles skirted the old question of whether an impeachable offense was necessarily a violation of law or just any form of malfeasance. Among the eleven were some charges that might gain the support of moderate senators unwilling to convict for general political obstructionism. The trial itself would reveal the dichotomy between legal and political considerations, which, however, could hardly be separated. Chief Justice Salmon Chase presided and tried to keep the Senate aware of its judicial function, though not always with success.

Presentation of the case taxed the abilities of the lawyers on both sides. The Managers, representing the House, were Congressmen Stevens, Butler, Boutwell, Thomas Williams, and John A. Logan of the radical faction and Wilson and John A. Bingham of the moderates. The President chose a stellar array of counsel. Henry Stanbery resigned as Attorney General to participate so there would be no charge of his compromising his position as chief legal officer for the government. Benjamin Curtis was a former Supreme Court justice and one of the two antislavery dissenters in the Dred Scott case. William Evarts, a Republican whose politics did not always square with Johnson's, added considerable skill. Thomas A. R. Nelson was an old Tennessee acquaintance. Ohio attorney William Groesbeck replaced Jeremiah Sullivan Black, who resigned in a huff after Johnson refused to accommodate him in a matter involving claims to a guano island in the Caribbean.

Appearing by counsel rather than in person taxed Johnson's patience. Often he savored the notion of striding into the chamber to do battle with his adversaries, and Moore noted that on several occasions he almost went. Cooler heads prevailed, however, and Johnson stayed away. He even agreed, under duress, to stop giving audiences to reporters during the trial. Whenever the defense did not conduct the trial as he thought best, he complained, as when Butler called him a murderer and a robber of the treasury and Evarts in reply merely called Butler's speech a "harangue." Said Johnson scornfully, "I believe he thinks he did a most smart and dreadful thing when he so termed Butler's reference to me." Johnson did not have much reason for concern, however, because his case was in excellent hands, and though the defense counsel had an uphill battle at first, they proved more capable than the Managers.

On March 16, while the defense was preparing its case, Stanbery came bouncing into the White House library and enthused, "Mr. President, you will come out all right. I feel it in my very bones. Do not lose a moment's sleep but be hopeful. We are bound to come out right." (His bones were benefiting from the twice-a-day services of a masseur.) Stanbery saw the trial as a golden opportunity to lay Johnson's whole official life before the country for examination and to compare his policies with those of the radicals. This, however, did not become the dominant theme of the defense. As the trial progressed, his lawyers did exactly what good defense lawyers ought to do when they have an unsavory client. They did not depict him as a helpless martyr of a radical conspiracy, which would have been unavailing as well as inaccurate. Instead, they concentrated on narrow legal issues and exploited the divisions among Republican senators. This intention became evident on March 23 when counsel read the President's responses to the eleven articles.

Johnson claimed that the Tenure of Office Act was unconstitutional, that in any case it did not cover Stanton, who had been a Lincoln appointee, and that Lincoln's "term" ended long before the removal. The President also claimed that full power to suspend or remove a Cabinet officer belonged to him under the Constitution, under the statute of 1789 that created the War Department, and under a 1795 statute covering vacancies in office. Furthermore, this full power of suspension or removal had long been a recognized feature of American history. He also asserted that since he had to remove Stanton and since no method had worked, he wanted his final actions on February 21 to produce a Supreme Court test of his power under the Constitution.

The various conspiracy charges Johnson easily denied. Article X he met by citing his freedom of speech as an American citizen and also his presidential prerogative to discuss political and constitutional issues in a public forum. The charge, in Article XI, that he had said Congress was an illegal body with no binding legislative authority, Johnson turned aside by noting that he had approved a great deal of legislation on all kinds of subjects passed by the same Congress.

On March 30 Butler began for the Managers, and prosecution testimony continued through April 4. After a short adjournment, Curtis opened the defense with a two-day argument, and testimony continued until April 20. As the trial progressed, it became apparent how carefully the defense had selected its ramparts. Since the Senate had repassed the Tenure of Office Act over the veto, arguing its constitutionality *per se* was fruitless. Yet Stanton, the object of all the fuss, had himself considered it unconstitutional and had spoken strongly against it at Cabinet, so much so that Johnson asked him to help write the veto. Though the point was hardly decisive, it did embarrass the opposition.

The nature of the removal power offered more ammunition for the defense. They argued that since the appointment power involved the Senate, it amounted to a specific exception to the general principle whereby the Constitution had confided the executive power to the president alone. It followed that since the Constitution was silent on removals, they were strictly the affair of the president. Congress had first been through this whole question in 1789 when it created the Department of State, and there the Madisonian view prevailed: the president could oust the secretary by himself. Madison, having been at the Philadelphia convention, carried as much authority as anyone, though Hamilton argued in *The Federalist* that removal was incident to appointment and thus a shared power. Actual practice from 1789 to 1867 upheld Johnson's position; in any event, it was difficult to maintain that the President ought to have to keep a high-ranking executive adviser in whom he had lost confidence.

The defense counsel spent even more time insisting that the Act did not even apply to Stanton. Unclear at the time of drafting, the issue was no clearer at the time of the trial. In 1867, House radicals definitely wanted the Cabinet and especially Stanton protected; Senate moderates opposed inclusion of the Cabinet. The awkward phraseology that resulted was intended as a compromise, and both chambers thought their positions had prevailed. Senator John Sherman, a principal architect of the law, and others believed Stanton was not covered, and the confusion would weigh heavily in the minds of those trying to be conscientious about legal detail.

The conspiracy articles amounted to very little by themselves, and the article condemning Johnson's speeches was weaker yet as an impeachable offense. Article XI, because it linked the events of February 21 into a two-year antilegislative campaign, finally seemed to the Managers to be the strongest article, though it really amounted to a summary of the others.

One other point had great significance, however, and that was Johnson's motives for ousting Stanton the way he did. If indeed he had concluded that only a court test could resolve the question of his presidential power, should the step taken to precipitate the test constitute an impeachable offense, especially when it would have been difficult to obtain such a test without an apparent violation of the act? The Managers thought the point sufficiently dangerous that they sought to exclude Cabinet members who could testify that Johnson intended a court test. Indeed, during the trial itself Congress showed that it considered the Supreme Court a potential ally of the President by passing a law removing the Court's appellate jurisdiction in cases where someone convicted by a military commission petitioned for release on a writ of *habeas corpus*. Such cases offered a clear opportunity to declare the Reconstruction Act unconstitutional. Of the Republicans who finally voted not guilty, John B. Henderson, James Grimes, and Edmund Ross took especial offense at the way the Managers had tried to stifle the issue of motive.

Final arguments began on April 22 and concluded on May 6. As this phase began, Moore was "perplexed" about what outcome Johnson expected, for the President apparently made no predictions. His spirits certainly had their low points during the trial. In early March he often paid daily visits to William Slade, his steward, who was dying of dropsy; later that month Moore noted, "The President dreads a return of his old trouble, gravel, and is not well tonight." In mid-April Johnson struck him as "unwell and gloomy." On April 20 the President sighed that "things seem to manage us instead of us managing them. I don't like it." As the arguments progressed, however, his spirits brightened, and on May 2 Moore noted a distinct change; three days later Johnson finally expressed his pleasure at the case and now even praised Evarts, who three weeks before had been too timid for presidential tastes.

Johnson should indeed have been pleased, for his counsel had done a superb job with a case that could easily have been botched had they allowed the Managers to control the style of the proceedings. But while the Managers attempted to sway wavering senators with appeals to partisan duty, the defense team stressed points of law and the murky issues, like the scope of the Tenure of Office Act, on which honest men could decide for acquittal as easily as for conviction.

Johnson himself provided a major assist during the argument phase. During the first week in April Senator Grimes, a Republican who believed the party's southern policy to be right but its impeachment program to be wrong, approached Johnson through Democratic contacts. Whether or not he spoke by commission for anyone else, Grimes suggested that if the President nominated an attractive candidate to replace Stanton, it would improve his standing with senators who found impeachment increasingly objectionable. Grimes also expected assurances that after the trial Johnson would not do anything precipitous or illegal, and he wanted satisfaction from the President personally. A dinner party offered a convenient occasion, and Grimes came away satisfied, which likely helped in the conversion of several other disaffected Republicans.

The result was that on April 21 Evarts asked General John Schofield, commanding in Virginia, to take the War Department. Schofield had ability and reputation and was the mildest Republican of the original five district commanders. Johnson gave up nothing, either, for he had never intended anything unlawful, and he made no promises to Grimes he could not keep. Most important, he did not initiate the contact; that a

Republican senator suggested the acceptability of a replacement for Stanton ratified in some degree his own position. Seen in this light, it was hardly a "deal" for acquittal.

After the summary arguments the Senate considered voting procedures and held closed-door meetings to discuss the evidence. Rumors had a dozen Republicans in the doubtful column, and the list changed every day. By May 16 the Senate was ready to vote. Excitement mounted to fever pitch. Admission tickets for the galleries could not be had at any price. Betting on the outcome was brisk. For Washingtonians, all eyes to the capitol was the watchword; for more distant Americans it was all ears to the telegraph offices.

The Chief Justice called the Senate to order, and by prior agreement the voting began with Article XI, apparently the strongest. Since the question had to be put in a particular form, the roll call went on almost interminably. When the clerk reached the letter V and West Virginia's Peter G. Van Winkle voted not guilty, the necessary thirty-six for conviction was impossible. Ben Wade, whose position as president *pro tempore* of the Senate would have brought him to the White House upon conviction, voted guilty, but by that time his vote made no difference. It merely intensified the question of who had committed the greater impropriety by voting at all, Wade or Tennessee's David Patterson, Johnson's son-in-law. A special telegraph line flashed the word to Willard's Hotel up the avenue, whence a courier ran it to the Executive Mansion. "The President took the matter very coolly," said Moore, "exhibiting no excitement, and receiving very pleasantly the many persons who called to tender their congratulations." The vote was 35 to 19, one short of conviction. Seven Republicans, Fessenden, Fowler, Grimes, Henderson, Ross, Trumbull, and Van Winkle, had voted not guilty; contemporaries believed four more would have done so if necessary to save the President.

After the vote the Senate adjourned for ten days before attempting the other articles. The recess allowed the impeachers time, by methods civil and uncivil, to seek the support of the seven wayward Republicans, but it also accommodated the Republican National Convention, which to nobody's surprise chose Grant. On May 26 the Senate reconvened. This time Articles II and III, which involved the appointment of Thomas, each produced another 35 to 19 tally, with the same rosters of names. There being no other article that might produce a better result, the Senate adjourned as a court of impeachment. Welles told his diary, "The Cabinet were all present with the President when the various votes were announced. His countenance lightened and showed a pleasant and satisfied smile, but the same calm, quiet composure remained. He had never believed otherwise than in acquittal."

A variety of causes brought about the result. The Managers clearly alienated some senators with their partisan demands and abrasive manner. Fessenden, Grimes, and others among the acquitting Republicans disliked Wade intensely and saw Johnson as the lesser of two evils. Wade also had inflationary financial views, whereas Johnson's congressional record on such issues inclined him to more cautious policies. Chief Justice Chase believed impeachment to be unwise, and his rulings on admissability of evidence and on procedural questions often helped the defense.

Larger legal and constitutional issues played a major role. Johnson, for all his opposition to Congress, had simply not done anything to warrant removal. The law he allegedly violated was so defective that even its sponsors could not agree on what it covered. His intentions also counted in his favor, for one of them, to get rid of a personally and officially unacceptable subordinate, might well be his prerogative as a man and a chief executive, while the other, to test the constitutional extent of his executive powers, might well be an appropriate step within the system of balance of powers. At least it was clear from the written opinions of senators who voted not guilty that these broad issues were legitimate, that where the weakness of the case itself gave rise to doubt, it was preferable to give the President the benefit thereof.

Of course, those who voted to convict had their own interpretations of separation of powers and the nature of an impeachable offense. Some truly believed that Johnson had violated the law; others that, even if he had not, impeachment for political opposition was appropriate. The "intentions" of the framers, always sought by both sides in such arguments, were less than decisive.

The actual precedents were no better. Of the five previous impeachments, only four came to trial (the Senate in 1799 decided that for jurisdictional reasons it had better not try one of its own members, the rascally Tennesseean William Blount, though it did expel him), and the four were rather disparate. Poor old Judge John Pickering had roared and lurched about in his New England courtroom in a drunken stupor, threatening to cane the refractory into submission, be they onlookers or participants. Hardly criminal behavior, this—but how else could one get a hopelessly demented judge off the bench except by impeachment? That he was a rock-ribbed Federalist at a time when some equally partisan Jeffersonians had just taken over the federal government did not help his case. Judge James Peck had survived weak and politically motivated charges in 1831, and Judge West Humphreys of Tennessee lost his seat in 1862 for disloyalty. Most significant among the whole mismatched lot was the case of Supreme Court Justice Samuel Chase in 1805. Without charging a violation of law, the Jeffersonians took him to task for conducting his office in a highly partisan fashion, particularly during trials under the Sedition Act.

Chase was acquitted, however, and that result gave precedence to a narrow concept of impeachment that lasted until the trial of Andrew Johnson. After Chase's acquittal the country simply lost its taste for impeachments that were primarily partisan, regardless of what argument and research might read into the phrase "high crimes and misdemeanors." Had it not been so, John Marshall would have been a very short-lived Chief Justice, and the articles of impeachment proposed against John Tyler, some of which resembled those against

Johnson, would have passed the House. Some of the senators who acquitted Johnson were saying by their votes that the country ought not to return, at the expense of the presidency, to a view of impeachment that the acquittal of Chase had cut off. After the acquittal of Johnson the narrow view of impeachment prevailed through proceedings against a cabinet member and five federal judges. In the case of Richard Nixon, warfare between executive and legislature over presidential power again provided a context, though in this case not the occasion, for charges involving specific violations of law and of the Constitution.

The country survived the demise of Nixon even though television newscasters inserted the phrase "constitutional crisis" into nearly every paragraph of copy. The country survived the impeachment of Johnson even though participants thought they, too, faced a constitutional crisis. Yet ultimately, in each case, both sides allowed the constitutional mechanisms to work through to a solution. As often happens in the American system when the legislative and executive branches disagree over the uses of power, the solution of 1868 was an accommodation. With the help of its constitutional protections, the presidential office withstood a direct legislative threat, even though, as the final year of Johnson's tenure ran its course, he and Congress continued to pursue the same views on Reconstruction and to exercise much the same powers as before impeachment. During the summer Congress accepted the results of its southern program and readmitted all of the states except Virginia, Texas, and Mississippi, where the program was not yet complete. Johnson, still insisting that the procedure was wrong, vetoed the measure, and Congress overrode. The Fourteenth Amendment, capable of working changes in the federal system that would only gradually become obvious, went into effect in July.

Johnson extended two more blanket pardons to southerners, one on July 4 and another at Christmas. The first still excepted those under indictment for treason or other felony (which meant Jefferson Davis), though Johnson did not want to, and agreed only after long discussion. The last one wiped the slate clean.

As for military power in the South, the army's duties there diminished upon readmission, but troops still kept order at election time and aided law enforcement officers. Stanton having resigned upon Johnson's acquittal, the Senate then confirmed Schofield, and Grant was still Commanding General. Johnson, however, continued to demonstrate his intention to be Commander-in-Chief, even to the extent of ordering his ultra-Democratic friend General Lovell Rousseau to the Louisiana command in September.

The President continued to lecture Congress on constitutional philosophy, and the amendments he proposed in July, though hardly new with him, now had rather an ironic political quality: direct election of senators and direct election of the president for a single six-year term.

The country could live with Johnson for his last year. Indeed, it had lived with him remarkably well for the previous three despite the common currency in wild passions, threatening rhetoric, and bizarre rumor that circulated in parlor, street, and chamber. The quarrel over power affected only the southern question. Johnson vetoed (by message) twenty-one measures during his term; only four of them, two in 1866 and two in 1869, had no relation to Reconstruction. They were minor bills and the vetoes stood. Of eight additional measures that he pocket-vetoed, one bore upon Reconstruction. A total of 364 presidential messages, responses, and transmittals on everything from the location of navy powder magazines to a commercial treaty with the queen of Madagascar formed a matrix of the ordinary against which the southern drama raged.

A more amicable relationship over Reconstruction might have enabled greater progress in other areas. Yet the United States did acquire Alaska, saber rattle the French into submission in Mexico, build railroads, mine gold and silver, police the frontier, expand national productivity, and attend to everyday things while the struggle went on. While Johnson offered no outstanding leadership in these areas, neither did he hold up non-Reconstruction measures to get his own way on southern policy.

The accommodation, however, was not entirely satisfactory, and one measure of how unsatisfactory it was occurred at the Democratic National Convention in July. On the evening of July 2, Moore and Johnson spoke about the nomination for the first time when the secretary remarked that he hoped the convention would give Johnson the tremendous vindication of the nomination. "He [Johnson] said, 'Why should they not take me up? They profess to accept my measures; they say I have stood by the Constitution and made a noble struggle. It is true, I am asked why don't I join the Democratic party. Why don't they join me?' he asked in marked emphasis, 'If I have administered the office of President so well.' " Over the next several days Moore believed that Johnson worried more over the convention outcome than he had over impeachment. He received a handful of votes, largely from southern delegates, but even General Hancock, second choice to the unwilling Sherman among the military possibilities, received greater support. On July 9 Johnson learned that the convention had settled on New York's Horatio Seymour. According to Welles, "The President was calm and exhibited very little emotion, but I could see he was disturbed and disappointed. He evidently had considerable expectation."

Now the only expectations were of going home. Years of continuous service took their toll of health and stamina if not of ambition, and Johnson was happy to leave Washington. Even with all of his family there, the capital had never been attractive to him, and while Johnson could be a gracious host, the social obligations of his position were tedious. Eliza hardly ever left her second-floor suite now, but for one special occasion she did make the effort. This was a children's ball, held on December 29, 1868, to help celebrate Johnson's sixtieth birthday. The only adults present were the Johnsons, to host the children of senators, congressmen, and other officials. The affair combined a suitable level of formality with a bountiful spread of ice cream, cake, and other big delights for small stomachs. There were other social events, like the traditional New Years' reception, attended, remarkably enough, by Ben Butler, to whom the President cordially extended a hand, but not by Ulysses Grant, who left town rather than attend.

Indeed, the mechanics of transferring administrations in this case strained the resources of protocol. Grant announced that he would not ride in the inaugural parade with Johnson, which was perfectly all right with the Tennesseean. But should there be any public appearance by Johnson at all? Johnson solved the problem in his own quiet way. Before inauguration day he moved his family out of the White House and crated up all his papers and records for shipment to Tennessee. On March 4 he had the Cabinet meet him at the White House in the morning, where he remained at his desk, signing last-minute laws and other documents rather than going to the Capitol for such tasks, as was the tradition. Just after noon he shook hands with the Cabinet, got into his carriage, and drove away. Grant would shortly be coming up the avenue to take possession of the Executive Mansion. That he believed he deserved to live there and that he appreciated the elegance of the office and the mansion would be apparent. Whether he understood the executive part of his new job would be a subject for official comment by Andrew Johnson his next time in town.

X I

Tennessee and Beyond
1869–1875

THE HILLS and valleys of East Tennessee were beautiful in summer, with rich farmland nestled among the rushing currents of the Holston and French Broad. It was a simple country, with sights and sounds that Andrew Johnson loved. Well might he savor the approaching summer of 1869, for but seven summers were left to him. Yet, though idyllic, they could not pass in idleness, and Johnson ill concealed his desire to make a political comeback. Summers were for elections, and in 1869 he helped conservative candidates win the legislature and governorship. Would the legislature now elect Johnson to the Senate? He came within two votes of election on one ballot, and when one of his friends estimated that $1,000 apiece would deliver the final two votes, Johnson swore if such a thing occurred, he would personally expose the fraud. He lost by a final count of 55 to 51.

In 1872 came an opportunity of a different kind. Tennessee acquired an additional place in the House from the 1870 census, and rather than redistrict the whole state, the legislature made this an at-large seat. Johnson ran as an independent against a Republican and a Democratic ex-Confederate general. For only the second time in his life Johnson lost a popular election, as the Republican won, but Johnson at least had the satisfaction of foiling one of the rebel brigadiers, whose political aspirations he delighted in undercutting.

Johnson would rather have his old Senate seat back "than to be monarch of the grandest empire on earth. For this I live, and will never die content without." In the fall of 1874 he began to campaign for the other Senate seat, whose current occupant was William G. Brownlow, once a bitter Whiggish prewar Johnson enemy, next a handclasping Unionist wartime Johnson supporter, now a reembittered radical Republican foe. Brownlow's term was up in March 1875, and Johnson could think of no greater pleasure than returning to the chamber that had once tried him and taking the vitriolic parson's place to boot.

Johnson's chief rival was another starred Confederate, William Bate, and when Nathan Bedford Forrest came to town to lobby for his fellow soldier, Johnson quipped that if Tennessee really wanted a Confederate general in the Senate, she might as well send Forrest himself rather than a "one-horse general" like Bate. Johnson won the election. Even in the North people took note. The Democrats had not wanted him as President again, but in Buffalo the Democrats fired a 100-gun salute upon his election. Thurlow Weed commented that only a remarkable man "could have dug himself out of a pit so deep and so dark as that into which he had fallen." The *Nation* remarked that his "respect for the law and the Constitution made his Administration a remarkable contrast to that which succeeded it."

Those were Johnson's sentiments exactly, and he soon made an opportunity to say so himself. Back in the summer of 1869 he had visited Washington briefly and had told a reporter that Grant was "mendacious, cunning, and treacherous" and totally inept at government. "He lied to me flagrantly, by God, and I convicted him by my whole Cabinet." Now in the spring of 1875 Johnson would make the same points in the chamber where he had once received equal vilification from his own critics.

President Grant called a special session of the Senate for March 4. Johnson arrived to take the oath and found the galleries packed, his desk loaded with flowers, and a dwindling thirteen-man remnant of the original thirty-five convicting Republicans wondering how to make the best of an embarrassing situation. Death, retirement, and rejection had cut a swath into the ranks of friend and foe alike, and satisfaction at outlasting implacable enemies, together with sadness at the absence of gentle faces, commingled in a silent, tearful contest for control of emotions. Standing with Hannibal Hamlin, Lincoln's first running mate and now a fellow freshman again, Johnson took the oath from Henry Wilson, once a convictor and now Vice President. He accepted quietly the congratulations of friends and settled into his old rooms at Willard's Hotel. The session bade fair to be short, but perhaps an opportunity would arise to say a few things that Johnson thought needed saying.

On March 22 the occasion arose with a resolution to approve Grant's action in using troops to support the government of Louisiana, headed by William Pitt Kellogg and made up of a radical Republican coalition of native white scalawags, northern carpetbaggers, and blacks against Democratic attacks. Johnson took the floor and thoroughly censured Grant's policy. He called the action a "monstrous" effort to undermine free government and exalt military power and accused Grant of desperately seeking to ensure himself a third term with southern Republican electoral votes. Times had changed but little. In 1867, when radical Reconstruction got underway, Johnson was writing vetoes castigating the use of military power to enforce changes in southern society and politics against the will of southern whites. Now, in 1875, when radical Reconstruction was falling apart in one state after another — for Louisiana was only one example of an ongoing phenomenon across the South from 1869 through 1877 — he was making speeches about the same things. Even the people were the same, for Sheridan was back in New Orleans, sent there by

Grant in December 1874 to supervise the use of troops, and he was up to his usual level of irascibility, calling the state's white Democratic organizations "banditti" and getting called in return a tyrant, a Stuart despot, and a disgrace to the Irish.

One thing was different, however. In 1867 Sheridan was a hero for four years of fighting rebels, and the Republican plan of Reconstruction drew support from Americans who wished to see southerners punished and blacks have a share of economic progress and political fairness. Now, in 1875, Sheridan was a hero for ten years of fighting Indians, and the spirit of reform that underlay support for Republican Reconstruction glimmered low. Americans no longer wished to bear the growing burden that maintenance of Republican Reconstruction entailed. They were interested in new things.

Or were they old things? Andrew Johnson would have recognized some of them, like filling up the western spaces with homesteads a bit farther out of town from Dodge City, Waco, or Bismarck than anybody had ever put one before. The manifest destiny of the 1870s had its forebear in the 1840s, and Johnson found the same national grandeur in the second installment as he had in the first. It was still a process of a man making his living by the sweat of his brow, and Johnson always regarded that as a virtue with a timeless quality. Of course, the Civil War introduced new factors, and some of them, had Johnson lived another decade to see them develop, he might have found disconcerting. The Civil War and industrialization came to America in the same generation, and the industrial capacity that the war demanded now underlay national peacetime development. It could not simply be turned off once the war ended. Nor did Americans want to, for there were railroads to build, precious metals to mine, cities to construct, profits to be made.

In all of this, however, the common man, Johnson's yeoman or mechanic or artisan, could easily get swallowed up and cry for relief by government from those economic forces that bore most heavily on him. States tried their best to regulate these matters, but this was no longer the 1850s, when a little railroad ran from Memphis out a few miles into the cotton country. This was the 1870s, when the Santa Fe would soon be chuffing from California to Chicago. Even as reform-minded farmers organized themselves into granges and elected their own men to state legislatures, the problems still grew beyond state ability to control. An increasingly national economy required more and more national regulation.

The old problem was still around: the desirable function of government. During Johnson's prewar days this political problem had some social and economic undercurrents; during the 1870s and afterward economic conditions took on increasing importance. Indeed, had Johnson lived for one more political generation, he might well have been a Populist; if their cause of agricultural reform through protective legislation could not win him from his small-government views, nothing would.

However, Johnson died in 1875, at a time when the desirable functions of government were still in flux. The old that he understood and wished to preserve had not yet fully given way to the new. The Fifteenth Amendment, prohibiting states from witholding the vote on the basis of race, took effect in 1870, and for a few years blacks voted in the South in substantial numbers. In 1870 and 1871 Congress enacted laws to enforce this amendment and to break the power of the Ku Klux Klan, but in a series of decisions from October 1875 until 1882 the Supreme Court declared these statutes unconstitutional. Three days before Johnson took his Senate seat, the Civil Rights Act of 1875 became law. The last effort of Congress to extend equal rights to blacks, it provided equal access to "the accommodations, advantages, facilities, and privileges of inns, public conveyances on land or water, theatres, and other places of public amusement." This law fell in 1884. The Supreme Court had already, in 1873, in its first interpretation of the Fourteenth Amendment, given it a very narrow meaning, which, had it been maintained, would have precluded the enormous power shifts within the federal system for which the amendment was responsible by 1900 and which continue to dominate twentieth-century constitutional law.

By the time Johnson died, the South was regaining what it liked to call "home rule," or local control of domestic matters, especially race relations. The process would be all but completed within two years after his death, when the election of Rutherford B. Hayes ended federal intervention in southern politics of the type Johnson had criticized in Louisiana in 1875.

Johnson had always favored home rule. It meant the abandonment of blacks to the wishes of southern whites, but Johnson had never wanted protection of blacks to be a federal function, anyway. Yet he would have made a rather poor Redeemer, as the native white southern Democrats who credited themselves with bringing about home rule called themselves. He shared their views on the law of race relations and social adjustment; otherwise, he was hardly their sort. They were planters who favored an economic alliance with factory owners and merchants and hoped to attract northern capital; he was still the champion of the yeoman and the mechanic. They sported their Confederate military service; he made no excuses for his Unionism. They had sometimes been Whigs before the war; he had always been a Democrat. They ignored the need of poorer whites for public education; he never gave up his support for schools. They condoned efforts to terrorize blacks to prevent them from voting; he did not. When he arrived in Washington to resume his Senate seat, he still had as much antipathy for the rebel brigadiers as he ever had for the prewar planter aristocracy and talked to friends about finding ways to control their power.

Whatever he might have had in mind, he took with him back to Greeneville that spring. He would not have a six-year term to work it out, however, for his seventh and last summer was at hand. On July 28 he took the train to Carter Station in the next county to visit Mary Stover and his grandchildren. After lunch he played for a while with little Lillie, and when she was leaving the room, she heard him fall to floor behind her, the victim of a paralytic stroke. The family got him into bed, and friends gathered. He could still speak, and he reminisced about years long gone. Another stroke left him unconscious, and in the small hours of July 31 he died. His family took him home to Greeneville where a large number of mourners, humble and prominent, turned out for the Masonic services and a procession through town to the spot on a little hill where he had planted a willow sprig descended from one at Napoleon's house on St. Helena. He had specifically asked to be wrapped in a flag and to have a copy of the Constitution beneath his head. It was done.

During the last train ride of Andrew Johnson's life through the Tennessee hills to Carter County he sat with an old friend who recalled Johnson's reflective mood. During his presidency, Johnson said, he had asked himself "more than a hundred times" what course he ought to follow so that the "calm" historian "one hundred years from now" would be able to say he had pursued the "right" course. As Johnson experienced more and more difficulty during his presidency, his concern with vindication by history increased. No president has ever put such considerations totally out of mind, and the president who looks too much toward his own future record may be blind to the needs of his national present. The other President Johnson, the Texan, observed in his television memoirs with Walter Cronkite: "The most difficult thing is not to do what is right but to know what is right."

Andrew Johnson always insisted he knew what was right. Doing it was never much of a problem either, in his own mind, although the tactics, the timing, the solitude, and the style made him a much more difficult individual than a president could afford to be. He had learned nothing from his congressional past about how to handle Congress as President. He never gave up a program whether it was popular or not. The art of compromise he never practiced except in a limited way on homesteads, and when during Reconstruction his friends urged him to do so, he could not. Here was a man, after all, who had publicly scorned the notion of compromise in 1850 when statesmen cried its necessity, yet he voted for more of the measures than most other southerners did because they were "right." As his later career demonstrated, that was not pose;

for him it was reality. The art of politics he had practiced only on a limited scale; in Tennessee the political reins offered a different tangle than those he found in Lincoln's White House. His early experiences had been more impressive on paper than in substance. The consitutional structure of power within a prewar federal system he understood well; in his later career he could not accept the pressures for shifts in the traditional alignment of federal and state power when they involved social and economic affairs in the South. Indeed, he was seeking to be a twentieth-century president but in quest of nineteenth-century goals, and in his quest he proved to be a prisoner of his own personal history. Theodore Roosevelt would have recognized the impulses toward a strong executive but would have thought the tactics questionable. Woodrow Wilson would have recognized the impulses toward insisting upon things that were "right," but he admired a parliamentary style of government far more than the Tennesseean did. Millard Fillmore would have recognized the America Johnson sought to preserve.

Summer in Greene County was a long road back from summer in the cities of urban America, and the vindication Johnson wanted from history is not history's to give or to withhold. What is history's to give is an explanation of how and why he followed the course he did, of the thoughts and actions that shaped his part in our national past. That is something which is never final, never infallible, never whole, and it is something we give not just to a historical figure but especially to ourselves.

A Note on the Sources

THE BIOGRAPHER of Andrew Johnson owes a large debt to the Library of Congress for preserving a large collection of Johnson manuscripts, available in a fifty-five-reel microfilm edition. From this collection and from many others LeRoy P. Graf and Ralph Haskins are compiling and editing, with meticulous care and insightful introductions, *The Papers of Andrew Johnson* (5 vols. to date, 1967–). Yet the quality of Johnson manuscript material is uneven. For the prewar years it is mostly incoming correspondence with some outgoing letters. Much of his own collection was destroyed during the war. For the presidential years the outgoing personal letters almost cease, and so one must rely on official documents and other sources.

All of the important prewar speeches and official papers are in Graf and Haskins, but the reader may also consult the journals of the Tennessee legislature for a record of votes and the appropriate volumes of the *Congressional Globe*. Some wartime correspondence is in the mammoth U.S. War Department, *The War of the Rebellion: A Compilation of the Official Records of the Union and Confederate Armies* (128 parts, 1880–1901), and in Roy P. Basler (ed.), *The Collected Works of Abraham Lincoln* (9 vols., 1953–55). Official presidential documents appear in James D. Richardson, *A Compilation of the Messages and Papers of the Presidents* (20 vols., 1897–1916). The government published the transcript of the impeachment trial, including written opinions by senators who chose to prepare them, as *Trial of Andrew Johnson, President of the United States, Before the Senate of the United States, on Impeachment by the House of Representatives, for High*

Crimes and Misdemeanors (3 vols., 1868). In addition, a great mass of documentary evidence regarding Reconstruction can be found in the serial set of congressional documents. Two handy compilations are Walter L. Fleming, *Documentary History of Reconstruction* (2 vols., 1907), and Edward McPherson, *The Political History of the United States of America During the Period of Reconstruction* (1875).

None of the existing biographies of Johnson is fully satisfactory. The early ones, narrative, anecdotal, and laudatory, are Frank Cowan, *Andrew Johnson, President of the United States: Reminiscences of his Private Life and Times* (1894), James S. Jones, *Andrew Johnson* (1901), and John Savage, *Life and Public Services of Andrew Johnson* (1866). There is also some biographical material in Frank Moore, *Speeches of Andrew Johnson, President of the United States* (1865). In the 1920s a new series of works appeared that were still highly laudatory. Lloyd P. Stryker, *Andrew Johnson: A Study in Courage* (1929), is much more polemic and less satisfactory than either Robert Winston, *Andrew Johnson: Plebeian and Patriot* (1928) or George Fort Milton, *The Age of Hate: Andrew Johnson and the Radicals* (1930), the last of which has the virtue of having specific references to oral reminiscences by people who knew Johnson. Another volume of the period, Howard K. Beale, *The Critical Year: A Study of Andrew Johnson and the Radicals* (1930), is scholarly, but its interpretation has been increasingly challenged. Lately Thomas, *The First President Johnson* (1968), is highly readable but relies heavily on the laudatory accounts of Winston and Milton.

In the 1960s, as scholars took a closer look at Reconstruction, Johnson came in for increasing criticism as the congressional Republicans rose above the ignominy to which writers on Johnson, and on Reconstruction generally, had consigned them during the first half of the twentieth century. For examples of these works the reader should see Eric L. McKitrick, *Andrew Johnson and Reconstruction* (1960), and LaWanda and John H. Cox, *Politics, Principle, and Prejudice, 1865–66* (1963). The present work's interpretation of the first year of Reconstruction accepts the Coxes' account of political maneuvering but not their reading of constitutional issues. For additional alternative views to the positions taken here, one may see William R. Brock, *An American Crisis: Congress and Reconstruction* (1963), Kenneth P. Stampp, *The Era of Reconstruction* (1965), Forrest G. Wood, *The Era of Reconstruction, 1863–77* (1975), and Michael Les Benedict, *A Compromise of Principle: Congressional Republicans and Reconstruction, 1863–69* (1974).

On impeachment the standard full-length account is David M. DeWitt, *The Impeachment and Trial of Andrew Johnson* (1903). Hans L. Trefousse, *Impeachment of a President: Andrew Johnson, the Blacks, and Reconstruction* (1975), is a modern, reliable account of the causes of impeachment to which, except for its disproportionate emphasis on racial issues, the present work is indebted. Michael Les Benedict, *The Impeachment and Trial of Andrew Johnson* (1973), questions DeWitt and argues that Johnson deserved impeachment, less on the specific charges than for general and deliberate obstruction of a desirable program. An assessment of impeachment generally in American history is Raoul Berger, *Impeachment: The Constitutional Problems* (1973). The historiography of earlier accounts of impeachment can be traced in James E. Sefton, "The Impeachment of Andrew Johnson: A Century of Writing," in *Civil War History* (1968).

Other recent works that the reader will find useful are Michael Perman, *Reunion Without Compromise: The South and Reconstruction, 1865–68* (1973), Martin Mantell, *Johnson, Grant, and the Politics of Reconstruction* (1973), Benjamin P. Thomas and Harold M. Hyman, *Stanton: The Life and Times of Lincoln's Secretary of War* (1962), and Hyman's article, "Johnson, Stanton, and Grant: A Reconsideration of the Army's Role in the Events Leading to Impeachment," *American Historical Review* (1960), James E. Sefton, *The United States Army and Reconstruction, 1865–77* (1967), Jonathan T. Dorris, *Pardon and Amnesty Under Lincoln and Johnson* (1953), Stanley Kutler, *Judicial Power and Reconstruction Politics* (1968), Charles Fairman, *Reconstruction and Reunion, 1864–88* (1971) (part of an uncompleted multivolume history of the Supreme Court), and Harold M. Hyman, *A More Perfect Union: The Impact of the Civil War and Reconstruction on the Constitution* (1973).

Andrew Johnson and Reconstruction continue to be sub-
jects of interest to doctoral candidates. Representative of the
dissertations undertaken in the last decade are Marshall Dale
Pierce, "Andrew Johnson and the South" (North Texas State
University, 1970), Hubert Bentley, "Andrew Johnson, Gover-
nor of Tennessee, 1853–57" (University of Tennessee, 1972),
Peter Maslowski, " 'Treason Must Be Made Odious': Military
Occupation and Wartime Reconstruction in Nashville, Ten-
nessee, 1862–65" (Ohio State University, 1972), William T. M.
Riches, "The Commoners: Andrew Johnson and Abraham
Lincoln to 1861" (University of Tennessee, 1976), and David
W. Bowen, "Andrew Johnson and the Negro" (University of
Tennessee, 1976).

For general Tennessee affairs one may consult Thomas P.
Abernethy, *From Frontier to Plantation in Tennessee* (1932), Stanley J. Folmsbee et al., *Tennessee: A Short History* (1969), James
W. Patton, *Unionism and Reconstruction in Tennessee* (1934), and
two volumes by Oliver P. Temple, who knew Johnson and gave
him grudging respect: *East Tennessee and the Civil War* (1899)
and *Notable Men of Tennessee* (1912). Johnson's governorship is
covered in two articles by Willie M. Caskey in *East Tennessee
Historical Society Publications* (1929 and 1930), his military governorship by Clifton R. Hall, *Andrew Johnson, Military Governor
of Tennessee* (1916), and the "swing around the circle" by
Gregg Phifer in a series of four articles in the *Tennessee Historical
Quarterly* (1952–53).

Four crucial diaries of the presidential years — when unoffi-
cial, personal expressions of Johnson's views are scarce — are
the notes of his private secretary, Colonel William G. Moore,
in the Library of Congress microfilm of the Johnson manuscripts and partially edited by St. George L. Sioussat in the
American Historical Review (1913), Howard K. Beale (ed.), *The
Diary of Edward Bates, 1859–66,* a volume of the American
Historical Association's Annual Report for 1930, Beale's *Diary
of Gideon Welles* (3 vols., 1960), which must be used cautiously,
and Theodore C. Pease and James G. Randall (eds.), *The Diary
of Oliver H. Browning* (2 vols., 1927–33).

To mention all the ephemeral journal and magazine articles

on some aspect of his life, some by scholars and many by people who knew Johnson, would be beyond the scope of this note. Many of them can be most conveniently located in the bibliography of Lately Thomas's 1968 biography, cited above. Likewise, a large number of biographies and memoirs of congressmen and other political figures contain useful insights. Many of these are listed in the bibliography in James G. Randall and David Donald, *The Civil War and Reconstruction* (2nd ed., revised, 1969), which also serves as an excellent guide to the vast literature on the middle period.

Permission to quote documents published in LeRoy P. Graf and Ralph Haskins (eds.), *The Papers of Andrew Johnson,* was kindly granted by The University of Tennessee Press. Permission to quote from Howard K. Beale (ed.), *Diary of Gideon Welles,* was kindly granted by W.W. Norton & Co.

Index